*"Untended fires soon die
and become just a pile of ashes."*

That simple statement was the practical, personal, and spiritual creed of a man who had eight decades behind him to support the truth of his words: If you want to sort out the priority issues of life, you start at the very beginning—with the "fire within." And until that matter is addressed, understood, and resolved, all attempts at easy answers in life will be absolutely fruitless. For a struggling young woman like myself, this was an insight of massive proportions... one that would prove to be the key to my attitude about living in "the fishbowl."

High Call High Privilege

❖ ❖ ❖

Gail MacDonald

LIVING BOOKS
Tyndale House Publishers, Inc.
Wheaton, Illinois

Living Books is a registered trademark
of Tyndale House Publishers, Inc.

All Scripture references are taken from the *Revised
Standard Version* unless otherwise noted. Other
versions quoted are *The Living Bible* (TLB), the
Moffatt Translation of *The Holy Bible*, and the *King
James Version* of *The Holy Bible* (KJV).
Living Books® edition
Library of Congress Catalog Card Number 87-50280
ISBN 0-8423-1349-4

Dedicated to

G O R D O N

my husband, pastor, teacher,
and best friend.
His daily choice to create
and to maintain conditions
for growth in our home
has made it possible for us
to experience great joy in our high calling.
This truly is our book. . . .

CONTENTS

PREFACE

THE possibility of this book being written began long ago when my husband was a young boy. His mother had repeatedly given him a high challenge, and he has remembered it well: "Someday, son, treat your wife like a queen."

There is no way that a pastoral marriage can be as rich as mine if the man who is husband has not first determined to treat his wife, as my mother-in-law once put it, "like a queen." I owe a deep debt of gratitude to my mother-in-law for having given my husband that advice, for I have benefited from it on a daily basis. In such a context I have been free to grow and have thus gained the courage and the confidence to write this book.

The possibility of this volume also emerged from our constant opportunity to closely relate to seminary students preparing for ministry. The questions and the concerns of soon-to-be pastors' wives have regularly prodded me to set forth a practical book of encouragement that might address some of the common issues of the pastor's family. As with so many of them, I, too, have searched over the years for specific and challenging information to help me on my journey in spiritual leadership.

But every time I looked, I found that too much was being

said about the woes of ministry and not enough about its privileges. I hope that my willingness to be vulnerable and to reveal the ministerial life that Gordon and I have shared will encourage many in Christian leadership to press on with new resolve in this matter of a high calling. If that happens, I will be most grateful.

No author can accomplish the task of writing alone. There must be a host of supporters who pray, stimulate thought, and push when the going gets rough. I want to thank Dianne Stephens, my husband's secretary, for spending many hours beyond her normal job load to type the manuscript. And I will always be grateful to two women, Shirley Clemmer and Jan Carlberg, who constantly affirmed me and my work. Without them, I suspect I would have occasionally laid my writing aside.

Then there are the people of the three congregations that my husband and I have served. I want them to know that the insights I've written about were acquired in the midst of their gracious fellowship. And finally, Gordon and I want to express our appreciation to the wonderful people at Tyndale House for their constant attention and regular prodding to encourage us in our writing endeavors.

Canterbury, New Hampshire, and Lexington, Massachusetts

INTRODUCTION

I WANT to make it perfectly clear at the outset that I do not consider myself to have "arrived" when it comes to this task of living in the circle of spiritual leadership. That fact is incontestable; the evidence, often damaging. Take, for example, a bad moment in my recent memory.

When I had gone to bed that night, my inner spirit was as dark as the sky outside. Swirling within me was the conviction that I was a failure, that the future was bleak, and that this lifestyle of ministry had become too much for me. What had happened that day? A special relationship had suddenly deteriorated into anger and hurt. What had made it so devastating was that the other person involved was a good friend. The events which had caused that breach were out of her hands and mine. Yet we were both suffering the consequences.

What a terrible and negative way to begin a book centered on the privileges and the joys of being in the ministry! But the fact is that what I experienced in that hour of despair is something understood and tasted by hosts of women in leadership or married to men who are. And such despair simply doesn't have to exist.

It's very important to understand the perimeters and the implications of our high calling. Moreover, if some of us do not trade notes on the insights we've discovered from scripture, from the history of the church, and from one another, we will all, sooner or later, fall victim to the same anguish that almost destroyed my own spirit that night.

In order to share my perspective on the subject of the life-style of women in leadership, I want to peel back the layers of the primary relationships in my own life and present some principles which I've gleaned and attempted to implement.

For me, key relationships emerge in five aspects of my experience. The first relationship focuses on my knowledge of, and closeness to, God. Without some awareness of the progress of that one, all other relationships in my life are up for grabs.

And while it may sound odd, I believe the second relationship of major importance is the one I have with myself. Self-awareness and a sense of self-worth are quite essential. Having placed those two relationships in that deliberate order, I then affirm my relationship with Gordon, my husband of twenty years. And that, of course, gives way to the fourth dimension of my relationships—that of being mother of two teenagers, Mark and Kristi.

A fifth relationship takes me out of the home and into the life of our congregation and community where I join my husband in the disciplines and pursuits of the pastoral ministry.

In writing about each of these relationships, I've tried to be honest—as much as possible. Also at every point I have tried to maintain an awareness of what might be called the "treasure-clay pot" balance. The Apostle Paul wrote to the Corinthians about his own sense of ministry:

> We have this treasure in earthen vessels (2 Corinthians 4:7)

or clay pots. It was his way of saying that we, as human beings, are relatively inexpensive and quite fragile containers, but God has poured *into us* the treasure of his gospel: the work of the Holy Spirit and the glory of Christ.

Portions of this book may appear to be idealistic, but only because I believe that too much emphasis has recently been placed upon the "clay" in our lives and not enough upon the "treasure" God invests in those eager to serve him. Some, in the relentless pursuit of so-called honesty, have overlooked the reality of what Paul called "treasure." Basically, in discussing the image of the "treasure and the clay pots," I don't want to emphasize one at the expense of the other!

My writing is directed to young women who are contemplating entering spiritual leadership, either as a single or a married person. I am also writing to young wives whose husbands are progressing through the rigors of a seminary curriculum and have been wondering what the world of Christian ministry will be like. Last but not least, I'm writing to a host of compatriots who, like me, are in the heat of spiritual battle at this very moment. Among them are the exhilarated and the discouraged. They will doubtless relate to many of the feelings and events which I've described. It is my hope that each reader will see her own uniqueness in God's design, never trying to be anyone else but herself—the person God intended her to be.

Perhaps as my description of the various relationships unfolds, you too will discover that bitter nights like the one I described earlier do not have to prevail in our lives. Even in those dark moments which will come, we can affirm that they are neither the terminus nor the norm of experience. Instead, they are growth moments from which can emerge a clearer vision of how to reflect the splendor of God and the joys of personal relationships. For all of us, can there be a greater privilege, a higher calling?

Part One

1
Come to the Fire

But see here, you who live in your own light, and warm yourselves from your own fires and not from God's; you will live among sorrows. (Isaiah 50:11, TLB)

EASY ANSWERS! They draw me as they do almost everyone else. I seek them instinctively in the books I read, the discussions in which I participate, and the speakers to whom I listen. I also confess to liking lists of do's and don'ts, simple statements that are measurable and can lead to some sort of personal success.

The problem is that I've chosen a lifestyle which does not lend itself to easy answers. Instead, I'm forced to think, to make difficult choices, and to face many different situations which often have no precedent. Thus I'm slowly learning that what I need are principles by which to think and to act; the easy answers are usually hollow and inadequate.

Years ago I chose to marry a man who would one day pastor three congregations. That choice meant that my lifestyle would be one of leadership often characterized by the unpredictable. In such an atmosphere, shortcuts, formulas, and rules would have been nice, but those simply would not hold up for the long haul.

I was on a search for easy answers the morning I sat in an enormous arena with thousands of other people listening to a retired missionary, an old man who was nearing his eightieth year and showed all the marks of a lifetime of spiritual warfare. *Perhaps a person twice my age will have some spiritual secret that I can press into my own life situation,* I thought. *Maybe he has one of those "easy answers" that will clear up some of those issues that have been burning inside of me.* . . . And so I strained to hear every word from a quivering voice weakened by the accumulated years.

But what I finally heard was neither an answer nor a rule. It was a *principle* placed in metaphorical perspective and destined to influence my inner life with God from that moment on.

I heard the old man quietly say, "Untended fires soon die and become just a pile of ashes."

That simple statement was the practical, personal, and spiritual creed of a man who had eight decades behind him to support the truth of his words. If you want to sort out the priority issues of life, you start at the very beginning —with the "fire within." And until that matter is addressed, understood, and resolved, all attempts at other easy answers in life will be absolutely fruitless. For a struggling young woman like myself, his was an insight of massive proportions.

Now I am well acquainted with life in the proverbial fishbowl. Having lived in it for almost twenty years, I understand more about pressure, applause and criticism, anger and joy, failure and success. And I'm also able to appreciate the stress which thousands of women experience daily as leaders among Christians or as women married to men in leadership.

Life in my own fishbowl has been an exciting experience. I wouldn't exchange it with anyone. Although there have been occasions in the past when I would have momentarily climbed out, the full effect for me has been one of great joy and thanksgiving.

I am aware that many are living in similar fishbowls, but without sharing my impression. For them fishbowl living has been painful and destructive, both spiritually and emotionally. Many would gladly trade it for an alternative style of life. And while there may be many different, even valid, reasons for such an adverse reaction, I believe that the special insight of tending the inner fire is the key to one's attitude about the fishbowl.

The principle of the untended fire lives with me on a daily basis now. It is my first thought when I come to my senses, realizing that the word I said an hour ago to a dear friend was misplaced and unkind. How could impatience and irritability have controlled my voice in that moment? The answer: The fire within had been left to dwindle.

Why do I find myself resisting the prompting to cross the fellowship hall in our church building and share a word of encouragement with a person I suspect tends to use sickness as an attention getter? Does it stem from the state of my fire within?

And what part of me glares at the telephone which has rung in our home for the "forty-eighth time" in the same morning? Is it the part that hasn't been recently warmed by the fire within?

The elder missionary's word about the fire has helped me to understand some of the special mysteries of the inner spirit. It has also helped me to see Jesus Christ as the great "fire-starter" who invites a woman like myself to a place of warmth in the same way he beckoned his confused and exhausted disciples to an early morning campfire on the shore of Lake Galilee. As they stood around the fire which he had started and tended, several things happened. They were fed; they were affirmed; they were instructed and commissioned to ministry.

And you could say that after that moment, the fire on the shore was strangely transferred to their innermost beings. And as long as they were willing to keep that fire tended, the fire burned within. The feeding, the affirming, the instructing, and the sending went on and on. I am slowly learning that every woman's life has to begin at that same sort of fire.

It has been some time since the missionary shared his principle, and I have freely embellished upon it with my own perceptions. But I have no doubt that he would agree that the fire must burn, not only within us, but also among us. And the central secret that determines the effect of its burning is in the choice to tend that fire, to keep it burning. If it burns brightly, we share the experience of the disciples; if it dwindles untended, life is gradually surrounded by a chill marking the onset of weakness and general confusion.

Since Christ is the "fire-starter," the fire had to be first within him. A simple study of his earthly life and ministry will underscore the fact that *he always tended first to the fire within himself.* In other words, he intimately communed with his own heavenly Father. Alert to that priority, Oswald Chambers once wrote:

> Our Lord's first obedience was to the will of his Father, not to the needs of men: his obedience brought the outcome of the saving of men. *If I am devoted to the cause of humanity only, I will soon be exhausted and come to the place where my love will falter;* but if I love Jesus Christ personally and passionately, I can serve humanity though men treat me as a doormat.[1]

Chambers and the old missionary have grasped the point. The issue does begin at the fire. The fire is the inner place of meeting with him. Jesus established that for us, both by his own response to the fire and his calling each of us to receive the fire he seeks to start within us. It's a principle, and there are no easy answers that supersede it. I've slowly figured that out! And for me it conveys the absolute conviction that a woman cannot survive in the fishbowl if she doesn't stay close to the fire and keep it tended.

My own pilgrimage with that fire has been a lifelong experience. Since earliest childhood days I had possessed a general hunger to be in touch with God. I didn't understand what I was searching for until, as a young teenager, I was invited by a boyfriend to a youth prayer meeting. I'll never forget my first impression when I saw a group of my peers on their knees, speaking personally to the God whom I'd been seeking. Soon after, I made a quiet, youthful commitment to Jesus Christ.

But what Christians often call *conversion* does not by any means imply *completion;* that soon became evident in my experience of spiritual growth. The young man who'd invited me to the prayer meeting became a steady boyfriend. Our relationship was a good one in that it caused me to pursue deeper Christian growth. However, it was unhealthy in that I confused commitment to Christ with dependence upon the boy whom I deeply admired. In solitary moments I had the feeling that my spiritual strength depended more upon a boy I felt I loved than upon Christ whom I'd accepted as Lord and Savior.

Looking upon our relationship, I now realize that I had been relying upon a human being to give me something that was humanly impossible for him to give. I was looking for a man to start the spiritual fire and to tend it for me. He couldn't and no one else could have either. The more I missed that point through immaturity, the more I clung to him in the hope of finally tapping a strength I thought he could surely transfer to me.

Understanding my unreasonable demands upon him has helped me appreciate what happens when people attempt to draw that same kind of strength *from me*. Surely, they reason, Gail has something (she's the pastor's wife, isn't she?) from which we can profit—if we draw close enough to her to get it.

When someone attempts to draw that kind of strength from me, I realize that while the person's motive may be good, the method is faulty—just as mine once was. That person needs to understand that she is relating to me as a *role* (the pastor's wife) rather than simply as a person. Some think that it's actually possible for me to share my fire, but what they need to know is that God's plan is to start a fire *within each of us*.

I fully appreciate what Henri Nouwen is saying when he writes:

> When we expect a friend or a lover to be able to take away our deepest pain, we expect from him or her something that cannot be given by human beings. No human being can understand us fully, no human being can give us unconditional love, no human being can offer constant affection, no human being can enter into the core of our being and heal our deepest brokenness. When we forget that and expect from others more than they can give, we will be quickly disillusioned; for when we do not receive what we expect, we easily become resentful, bitter, revengeful and even violent.[2]

What happened to me in my early Christian years dramatically illustrates what Nouwen has expressed so well. I had been expecting what another could not give. I wanted to be warmed at the fire which my boyfriend tended and fueled for himself. My desire was unfair and impossible.

Today I am slow to judge people who make that same mistake. When that mistake once threatened to destroy me, I faced the temptation to become, as Nouwen warns, bitter, resentful, and revengeful.

What finally happened? After graduating from high school, my boyfriend and I became engaged. At the end of freshman year at Taylor University, we decided that I should drop out to earn the money that would make both marriage and his continuing education a possibility. By summer's end he returned to the campus; I got a job. Soon a bank account began accumulating and a hope chest began filling up. Honeymoon reservations were made, and wedding plans crystallized smoothly.

But one day, as the wedding date approached, a shocking letter came from my fiancé at college. He wished to terminate the relationship—abruptly, decisively, without explanation. It was over! I never saw him again!

Loss, confusion, rejection, and self-pity engulfed me as I grieved alone in my bedroom. My parents were sensitive and allowed that time of grief. Three years of my life suddenly seemed null and void.

In retrospect I see that I had two alternatives: falling into the trap that Nouwen warns about or squarely facing the weakness of my own dependent position and choosing a path that would maintain a growing fire within myself.

The turning point came a few days later when my father poked his head into my room and said, "Well, honey, I guess we're going to find out whether or not this Jesus is really all you've been trying to tell us he is to you."

If they were not comforting words, they were certainly challenging ones. And they were exactly what I needed to escape from a prison of self-pity. From that moment on I resolved to tend my own fire, the one Christ had started. I'm not sure what my father had in mind when he made his blunt comment, but I will be forever thankful for his intrusion on my mood. It made me determine to act on my own for once.

It was important for me to do something immediately. Returning wedding gifts, contacting my ex-fiancé's parents, cancelling honeymoon reservations, and explaining the situation to friends were painful activities. But they were a beginning point in my realization that Christ's fire could sustain me. It did in fact.

Despair, depression, and a generalized sense of confusion can often be handled when one sets out to create, at the least, a corner of life filled with resolve and control. Once a beachhead of that sort has been established, it is a matter of simply extending it into other parts of one's life. And that's exactly what I did.

I went on and did three other seemingly strange things.

First, I began a prayer meeting in our church, which hadn't had one for some time. Secondly, I began to visit lonely people in the hospital once a week. Hospitals had an ironic way of making me feel sick; I knew I had to overcome that psychosomatic reaction before I could really help others. Thirdly, I resolved to go back to college and finish my degree.

I must mention that the young man who broke our engagement went on to become a man of God. I'm not sure that he would have ever achieved the levels of maturity and accomplishment he attained had we fulfilled our intentions to be married. I am also not confident that I would have ever participated in his growth and development. Rather, I suspect that if there had not been a crisis of the sort I'd faced, I would have been a serious negative influence in his life. I would have drained his own fire of the power he needed for himself. You could say that my pain was his release.

But my pain was also *my* release. Those simple resolves I made filled my life with a new sense of meaning. As I made small, steady steps forward, I began to see spiritual progress—the growth of my own fire. My final three years (at the University of Denver) flew by quickly. The challenges of being a student and a resident assistant in the dormitories and of holding a part-time job in a local church began strongly shaping my future.

Drawing closer and closer to the fire Jesus Christ had started, I gained insights that have remained with me throughout the years of my adulthood. Of course there were the usual hurts, disappointments, and certainly failures. But through it all God was shaping me into a woman who could do something significant in her own little world.

It is no surprise now when I look back and see that God had a perfectly prepared timetable for my inner growth and my future relationships. After only five years of lessons and experiences, including growth in my personal relationship to God, he allowed circumstances to bring me into contact with the man destined to become my husband.

How can I adequately convey the mysterious joy that sprang up within me when I learned that his life was committed to ministry in the same way that I had already chosen to commit mine?

What we were to form was not simply *his* ministry, a kind of bandwagon for me to jump upon. Instead, it was the merger of *two* ministries independently commissioned by the Christ of the inner fire. Our marriage would be marked by prior visions of call and commission. All of that began twenty years ago.

Christ starts the fire and invites a person to join him. My experience tells me that he is more than willing to keep the fire burning brightly for a time, but that a process is soon set into motion in which he begins to hand over the responsibility of tending the fire to us. And if there is a continuing, tended fire, he'll be with us and will continue that heavenly whisper of comfort and challenge, of gentle rebuke and affirmation.

It sobers me to realize that many woman all over the world have entered the fishbowl as leaders or as wives of men who are in Christian leadership. Each of us is unique, and it would be a mistake to assume that all should feel intimidated to conform to one set "image."

But one thing all of these women should share is a kind of joy that erupts from knowing that God has privileged each of us to be a part of a life marked by servanthood. The fact is that many women do not have that kind of joy either because they've lost it or because they have never found it.

In the very early days of the ministry that Gordon and I had begun to share together, the wife of a pastor told me, "Gail, you're going to learn to hate the ministry." That comment shocked me! It seemed to clash with all my idealistic, romantic notions of what I'd thought life with my husband, the pastor, would become. Why would a woman, thirty years ahead of me, admit to such bitterness and distaste for something I'd been dreaming about for such a long time?

Why did she want to pour cold water upon the vision Gordon and I had fought so hard to achieve as we'd worked his way through seminary? Sadly she was not the last woman from whom I was to hear that familiar theme during the passing years.

Many things, of course, could have been implied in a statement like that. Here and there the wives of some Christian leaders have been victimized by circumstances and situations both painfully agonizing and unfair. They have been joined to husbands who were less than sensitive to them as persons and who often left them to fend for themselves. Such women have faced congregational problems that tore at the human spirit. And perhaps there are those who've lived with hardships which were the result of the sins of other people.

I believe that the majority of women for whom ministry has been an unhappy experience share a common problem. They have perhaps perceived neither the principle of the inner fire, nor its potential. They have consigned themselves to trying to make life work according to structures and external standards, but that's not the way to reach the fire! Thus, having missed the energy and the direction which comes from that fixed, centered experience, they attempt to live on an energy that comes from other sources. Sooner or later, stresses mount, crises occur, temptations arise. They then find themselves facing the lot of a fishbowl life and saying, "We've learned to hate it." Ministry is far too draining to be sustained without the experience of the inner fire.

Returning to the fire—where Christ is to be found—tending it, and learning to listen to his voice have not been easy for me. As long as I live, I fear that there will be times when a part of me will resist coming back because it is all too often a place which costs me my pride. Like everyone else, I'd like to think I can do some things alone. Also I'm not always keen to face up to the aspects of my being which are not reflecting the nature of God. The fire exposes those things. And again, conversation at the fire tends to point people in directions that they might like to avoid: unlikable people, responsibility, and mature inner attitudes.

My own trek to the fire, however, has brought me to some light-giving discoveries, straightedges, if you please, by which to measure my progress. I have come to discoveries that our Lord knew and lived out with his Father. Nothing new or novel, but I regard them as the essential keys to what makes life in the fishbowl an exciting experience. Because of them, I've learned not to hate the ministry (in spite of its exhausting routines) but rather to rejoice in the privilege, as the Apostle Paul put it, of being "counted worthy" to be part of God's sacred call.

2
The Mystery of Personal Disengagement

The bow that is always bent will soon cease to shoot straight.
John the Apostle

ON MY DESK lies an invitation to a conference. At the bottom of the invitation are the words: "This invitation is for the recipient only and is not transferable to any other person." In short, I can't send anyone in my place. Either I choose to attend for myself, or I refuse the invitation.

When Jesus Christ invites me to his fire, his invitation is nontransferable. In a special sense it is only for me. While others may go *with* me, none can go *for* me. And what happens at that fire? The same kinds of things that happened to Peter, John, and the others: self-examination, restoration, affirmation, recommissioning—an intimacy that fills and recalibrates the inner spirit.

Throughout the years of our ministry, my husband and I have occasionally felt on the edge of an ill-defined despair. Those were times when we felt a variety of things: a desire to either quit or run, a feeling of anger, the temptation to fight back at someone, the sense of being used or exploited, the weakness of inadequacy, and the reality of loneliness. Such attitudes can easily conspire to reduce the strongest and the most gifted to a state of nothingness.

During such dark moments, choices and decisions are often made which one may live to regret for years. That's why the invitation to the fire is so important. At Christ's fire false feelings, empty threats, and unpleasant attitudes are sorted out and replaced with healthy things. You might call it burnout, self-pity, bitterness, or simply plain old failure—regardless of what you call it, defeat exists in the majority of situations like this, because Christ's fire was ignored. Thomas à Kempis understood that when he said, "When a man begins to grow cold, then he makes much of a little labor, and seeks *outward* consolation." In other words, such a person seeks strength and solace from a source other than the fire, but it doesn't work!

While I've loved the patterns of my life, I have been aware that life is often similar to being inside a hurricane. I'm surrounded by the same stresses and trials other human beings face, and it would be easy to be caught up in those things. While it does happen occasionally, few people contact either Gordon or myself to share good news. We are more usually confronted with the bad side of things. We accept that; it's part of our call and the price we must pay to be part of the spiritual medical corps. We cannot resent the spiritual struggles that people face just as a physician must not resent the sickness his patients bring to him for diagnosis and treatment.

The key to living in the hurricane of human events is to *operate from the eye*. The eye is the center of the storm, the place of peace and of a type of normalcy. How do we stay in the eye of the storm? Through frequent visits to the fire of Christ.

Examining the lives of the early church leaders, of the prophets, and of the holy men and women of Scripture can help make sense out of that answer. However, Christ himself and his relationship to his heavenly Father gives the most impressive example. Certainly Christ's life was surrounded by hurricanelike winds and forces, yet they never deterred him from his priorities or his sense of mission! He was never unnerved and never responded in a way that was out of line with his character. How did he maintain such composure? How did he operate from the eye of his own personal hurricane?

The answer, I believe, is simple but profound: *He had a fire of his own.* Call it the "Father's fire," to which Jesus retreated with regularity. When he returned from such personal encounters, he was prepared to face the rigors of the new day.

I often recall a particularly draining day Jesus faced at Capernaum. As the day wore on, the momentum of ministry increased with long lines of people apparently coming to ask for healing, counsel, and liberation from demon possession. Doubtless, Jesus felt consumed by the needs of the people and therefore exhausted.

Scripture says that Jesus withdrew that night into the mountains beyond Capernaum. While others slept, he prayed. Why? What was happening? His inner spirit needed restoration and filling far more than his body needed further sleep. In other words, he pursued a policy of *personal disengagement*.

Have you ever pondered the content of that night's conversation with the heavenly Father? Did some sort of inner debate take place as Jesus wrestled with his priorities and the excitement and the applause he'd received that previous day in Capernaum? Do you suppose he had to fight the temptation to spend greater and greater amounts of time in the healing ministry because that was what people obviously wanted? Was there that night a crisis of definition about his mission? Did he struggle over what was the best way for him to spend his time? Apparently the battle was won. The next morning Peter found him and said:

Everyone is asking for you. (Mark 1:37, TLB)

That was the opening word from a man who had slept well and had gotten up early the next morning to continue the previous day's successes. How shocked he must have been when Jesus refused to return to Capernaum, the place of massive public acceptance, and said:

> We must go on to other towns as well.... (Mark 1:38, TLB)

What accounts for the difference in their perspectives? Jesus had spent the night at the fire; Peter had slept. Their perceptions about what was right and essential were thus quite different the next morning.

What can women who choose to live in the hurricane—in the fishbowl, in the mainstream of needy people—learn from that story? That there must be a time of restorative withdrawal at the fire where Christ is. From it, energies are renewed, perspectives refocused, and directions newly defined.

Perhaps it seems ironic that I have been talking about serving people by first disengaging from them. Strange as it may seem, that is exactly where we must begin. Many ultimately fail because they don't begin there. Leaving the eye of the hurricane, they get sucked into the storm. Church tradition says that John the Apostle once observed, "The bow that is always bent will soon cease to shoot straight."

Paul Rees once urged me to "learn the rhythm of engaging and disengaging as our Lord did." I thought he was asking me to do the impossible.

"Do you understand," I asked him, "how busy I can get in this life of mine?" *Does he know,* I wondered, *the number of times the phone rings? Has he any idea of the demands my children make? Has he ever lived according to the church calendar and the well-meaning invitations that people expect me to accept?*

"Most certainly!" he quickly responded. He'd lived that way for years himself, he reminded me. "Besides, there'll never be a time when the noises of your world won't compete relentlessly for your attention," he warned me, much to my surprise. They would get so loud, he said, that they would usually drown out the quiet invitations of Christ to join him at his fire. I would simply have to choose early in my adult life whether or not to make tending Christ's fire a priority. No one would force me there, but I would learn later on that resisting it would end in a tragic loss for me.

Disengagement! Going to the fire. I must tell you that I soon discovered that virtually every part of my inner and outer life militated against my doing what Paul Rees said was most important. General noise, random events, demands of people, poorly organized schedules, inner turbulence, rebellion, and an inability to separate the good things from the best, these and many more ruthlessly tugged each day at my will and made going to the fire of Christ a difficult task. Frankly that struggle exists to this day. And when I give in to such demands and put Christ off, the result is frequently exhaustion (both physical and spiritual), loss of perspective, defensiveness, self-pity, and an absence of joy.

That's the sort of thing that Isaiah was speaking of when he wrote:

> They who wait for the Lord shall renew their strength, . . .
> they shall run and not be weary, they shall walk and not
> faint. (Isaiah 40:31)

Without the waiting at the fire, we become sapped. With it we seem tireless by contrast.

Disengagement means silence before God, first of all. It is a time of heavenly discussion during which we listen more than we speak. And silence demands solitude. Does it impress you, as it does me, that these are two matters which our world is substantially ignorant of and often seems to resist?

The ancient Desert Fathers used to commit themselves to a disciplinary creed: silence, solitude, and inner peace (*fuge, tace, et quiesce*). Only after adequate amounts of time listening, did they consider themselves ready to speak.

33

Without large blocks of silence and solitude, Gordon and I have found that we are in danger of losing the very best things that people desire to draw from us: fresh insights from God's Word, alertness to personal need, resources with which to encourage others, and a Christ-centered life-style which some might choose to emulate.

But what surprises both of us is that we've been criticized for seeking that very disengagement which makes us ultimately more useful and strong. One day a person told me, "You look exhausted! Are you getting enough rest?" A few weeks later, upon discovering that we had been away for a day, that same person said, "It must be nice to be able to do the things that you like to do."

We smile, knowing that few actually realize that our occasional withdrawal is ultimately for their good as well as ours. Not to rhythmically withdraw to Christ's fire will be finally to fail the people to whom Christ has called us to minister.

But frankly there have been many times when I have been defensive and super-sensitive. I wrote the following words in my spiritual journal:

> We have been with two couples today. One of the men was concerned about Gordon burning out, doing too much. The other subtly jabbed at him about the fact that pastors get four weeks' vacation, while in his "industry" men get only two. The contrast between the attitudes shocked and angered me.

My own spirit during that writing had obviously been needy. My response had been inadequate and showed a lack of perspective.

What voices do we listen to? We want to please those we serve. Thomas a'Kempis' words help untangle the dilemma:

> There is no great reliance to be placed in a frail and mortal man, though he may be helpful and dear to us;

neither should we be much grieved, if at times he should be against us and contradict us. Those who are with you today may be against you tomorrow and the opposite may be the case, for men often change like the wind. Place your whole trust in the Lord; let Him alone be your fear and your love. He Himself will answer for you and will do what is best for you.[1]

Saint Thomas understood the stresses that I live with. And from such a resource I am again reminded that while the critic's voice must be heeded, a louder word from God must be heard first. Our culture has not adequately taught us to appreciate the need for disengagement from anything except for personal leisure. Thus those of us in ministry should not expect a large number of people to understand our need to disengage. Moreover, we should not be surprised when we ourselves struggle with false guilt for having separated ourselves from our work.

During a time of withdrawal, it is all too easy for the spiritual enemy to impulse our minds with thoughts like "This is a waste of time" or "Action is more important than meditation" or "We are simply succumbing to laziness." Those are the inner temptations which, when combined with the outer ones, make our move to the fire a battle. But it is a battle which must be won.

Among many Christian women today, there is a strange sort of logic that suggests that spiritual resource and renewal are found in constantly seeking new voices, attending more meetings, listening to incessant music, and gathering to exchange half thought-out opinions. How often do we fall into the trap of believing that God is most pleased when we have maximized our information, our schedules, our relationships? Have we misunderstood the implication of fellowship and community? Do we fail to comprehend that these beautiful qualities of corporate life dwindle in value and substance when they are pursued by people who have not yet enjoyed intimacy with Christ?

Karen Mains' statement "I know more than I've experienced" is profound. When do we allow the truth we already know to percolate through our spirits and become part of our lifestyle?

When I have the privilege of speaking at a women's retreat, I make one request of those in charge. I ask that the women on retreat take two or three hours for silence and total solitude on the Saturday morning or afternoon of the retreat. Without exception, this has been a time when fires in many hearts have been rekindled. The voice of God has spoken to many in rebuke, comfort, and challenge. Relationships have been healed, and on many occasions hardened hearts have been broken.

Retreats can be so full of ideas and truth that many go home exhausted and depressed because they cannot live up to all they've heard. Why? Because there was no time for thinking or pausing to meditate upon ways in which the instruction could be helpful and could be implemented. Would Simon Peter have been so confident of his ability to follow Christ even to the cross if he'd taken some time to think through the implications of his promises for discipleship?

One of the women in our congregation gave us a beautiful word picture to describe the period of silence on a retreat. She likened it to "bonding," the moments just following the birth of a baby. The newborn is gently laid on its mother's tummy and gains strength from her closeness and warmth. After the rigors both have been through, what wordless comfort must exist there! We need a time for bonding with our Lord as well. If not, we will *know* more than we are living and become frustrated and negative.

It would be unfair for me to suggest that being nudged to the fire during those retreats has been welcomed by all. To the contrary, many have admitted dreading it. Others, thinking it a waste, have talked to each other instead, but are pleasantly surprised by the outcome. For many it is a first.

I come away from such retreats, believing my best gift to the women was the bonding time, not my talk. If the weather is good so that we can be outdoors, the effect has always been heightened. Better than a room with four walls, nature is alive and speaks restorative words to us, silent words of growth and dormancy, stability and weakness, flower and weed, health and decay, life and death, and patience in process.

Frequently when drained in spirit myself, I have spent a day outside, watching the birds, feeling the snow fall, listening to the Voice in the quiet, and dwelling on Scripture. Belonging to the life behind nature can't help but rekindle even the weariest of hearts.

If we are always in the city surrounded by buildings which are large but not alive, we'll feel dwarfed. We may marvel at what great engineering and architectural minds have done, but we can't draw life and strength from steel and mortar. We draw life from what is alive!

The biographer of Brother Lawrence once wrote of that holy man:

> In the winter seeing a tree stripped of its leaves, and considering that within a little time the leaves would be renewed and after that the flowers and fruit would appear, he received such a high view of the providence and power of God which has never since been effaced from his soul.[2]

Recognizing that it is Christ himself who "holds all things together," I see that same power possible in me and therefore through me to others.

The wife of a pastor said to me, "I've heard it all. I've been listening to sermons and Bible lectures all my life. I know everything my husband will say before he says it." Her frustration revealed more than she realized—that she'd been taking it all in but had not learned to give it out. Like a swamp, her inner spirit had become stagnant. If she tends

37

Christ's fire and begins to receive the recommissioning that points out how to give love away, she will also discover what spiritual gifts she has to make the giving of love most natural. At that point she will never grow tired of the things her husband might say.

Experiences at the fire will replace the swamp with a flowing river of service. And that in turn will make her hungry for those times when she can eagerly grasp more and more nuggets of truth which Christ can give her later. I talked with her further about the meaning of going to Christ's fire. By the time she left me, she had become committed to a new sense of discovery about what Christ might say to her.

There is mystery in disengagement. The mystery stems from the fact that what we do at Christ's fire seems to be the absolute opposite of everything our society has taught us to do. At the fire there is no busyness; we find only stillness and silence. At the fire there is the open ear of the heart and a world of possibilities for two people, a small attendance indeed. And the two? Christ and myself or Christ and you.

3
The Functions of Disengagement

Find the rhythm of engaging and disengaging as Christ did.
Paul Rees

"I'VE ACCEPTED the truth about the importance of disengagement. What happens next?" The question is a natural one. While I can share a few of my own answers, let me underscore the uniqueness of the experience and the fact that there are differences for each of us to pursue and to enjoy. I, for example, have found a rhythm of place, time, and method which works for me. It is all part of my single objective: to hear God speak to me.

One thing must be true for all of us. Of necessity, things like the phone, the radio, the TV, and the stereo must not be allowed to interrupt what begins to happen to us as we join Christ at the fire. Many special thoughts and insights may never return if we allow them to be interrupted.

Some have suggested that our appointment with Christ should be treated as any other appointment. If some sort of legitimate interference makes it impossible to meet with him, we should promise ourselves that it will be rescheduled for later in the same day. We should always be aware that this relationship is as important to him as it is to us.

Obviously Scripture is the central text for conversation with God. Most often I have looked at portions of the Word of God with a particular theme in mind. For example, I once did a study on the subject of inner confidence in Christ at a time when I had too little confidence myself. As I found a story or a passage which spoke to that particular theme, I would write it down in the back of my Bible to be recalled or shared with others later. On another occasion I studied the ways in which affirmation had been accomplished by Jesus, by the apostles, and by other spiritual leaders. I noted the differences between flattery and affirmation. The study made a significant contribution in my leadership relationship with others.

In times when my spirit has been drained, I have poured through the Scriptures, looking for references to the different attributes of God. Choosing one, such as *mercy,* I have listed all the different suggestions and examples of it as indicated in his Word. Studies on the subjects of love, deception, prayer, weakness, strength, the personality traits of various biblical men and women, and even Jesus' style of relating to women have meant a great deal to me.

In recent years, I have augmented my Bible reading with the insights of some of the great Christian thinkers: the journal of John Woolman; the thoughts of Fenelon, Brigid Herman, Thomas a'Kempis, Elton Trueblood; the biographies of people like Hudson and Maria Taylor, Sarah and Jonathan Edwards, and Henry Martyn; and the perspectives of Bonhoeffer, Henri Nouwen, and A. W. Tozer. These and many others ought to be carried to the fire as resources for added spiritual stimulation.

But nothing is ever more important at the fire than simply opening our inner spirits to let the Spirit of Christ speak directly. It makes little difference whether we are on our knees, walking, or sitting comfortably. However, there must be moments when we expel from our inner beings the negative thoughts, the rebellious attitudes, and the selfish patterns. Otherwise, how can we honestly ask Christ to refill us with his thoughts, his insights, his direction, and his love? This can only be done in silence. It seems obvious but bears repeating: We cannot follow his directions and insights if we have not lived in his Word to us.

Recently Gordon and I spent a treasured afternoon with a pastor and his wife who have been married for sixty-two years. Now at age eighty-five, they actively minister in the nursing home to which they have retired. They show no sign of self-pity, only delight in continuing to be useful and to comfort other people.

One thing was especially obvious to both Gordon and me—their intimacy with Scripture. The pastor's wife had so immersed herself in Scripture that it had become a spontaneous dimension of her speech. While the two of us visited, her husband and Gordon shared their knowledge of different Greek words and the fresh depth that the Greek had given to their understanding of Scripture. We were amazed that two eighty-five-year-olds still found it important to saturate themselves in holy Scripture and to enjoy fellowship through it with the Lord. Yet how can one be an eager, loving, positive servant of Christ at eighty-five without daily tending the fire at which Christ is present?

Gordon and I have learned the further discipline of keeping a spiritual journal. For over seventeen years we've kept separate notebooks charting the things that God has shown us through the Bible, through people, and through events. Feelings, struggles, and ecstasies have become a collage of experience describing how God has worked in our lives. Again and again we've been able to consult our journals and compare our feelings at certain times of the year or during an event that is similar to events we've faced before. What we've seen God do in the past has often become a great help in the present.

A journal has also been a tremendous help in recording prayers which I seem to have trouble thinking through in my mind. Writing helps clarify a feeling or an attitude which I can't quite verbalize. I wish that I could say that

I've written in my journal with daily regularity. I haven't. But even though there are stretches when I have lapsed in my encounters with the journal, what I do have has become invaluable.

In retrospect the most helpful journal entries have come during those longer periods of my being alone. I am reminded that Jesus took entire days for time with his heavenly Father. He accumulated long periods of silence and drastically changed his pace on many occasions. During similar times for us, astounding spiritual momentum can be developed. The inner part of us can begin to race with insight after insight as God's Spirit speaks to us about himself, ourselves, and our mission. A day at the fire can often provide energy for many weeks of leadership and ministry.

I can imagine the mother of young children becoming frustrated by some of my thoughts as she reflects upon the constant needs and interruptions she has to face. I certainly understand that tension because for many years I, too, wrestled with the reality of constant interruption. Still, short periods of meditation are possible throughout the day of a young mother. They can occur during a baby's nap or perhaps even late in the evening when a small child has gone to bed.

The perceptive husband will make sure that his wife has freedom for special moments by assuming responsibilities with the children for a period of time. Both marriage partners must see the importance of the fire experience if both are to remain healthy in spirit.

One thing remains certain: *We make a trip to Christ's fire possible by choosing to do it.* If we excuse ourselves by claiming that circumstances are too demanding, we have set in motion a pattern that will provide excuses for the rest of our lives. If we are too busy, something in the schedule should be sacrificed—not the time with Christ. He himself demonstrated that when he went to a fire that God made for him, others waited.

Recently I planned a visit to the hospital in the hope of

encouraging a friend of mine who would be undergoing brain cancer surgery. Before going, I sat at my kitchen table and reminded the Lord of Jacob's words:

I will not let you go, unless you bless me. (Genesis 32:26)

I asked the heavenly Father to clear my thinking and re-arrange my thoughts so that I could center on my friend's needs. Two hours later I was ready to go.

One of the thoughts which I believe came straight from heaven was to take a hymnal and choose songs of worship and comfort. That was something I'd never done before, but I found myself being prepared by worshiping through those hymns. Handpicked Scriptures were then chosen and claimed.

The time that my friend and I shared in the hospital affected my life as well as hers. I've since wondered what I would have given her had I chosen to go without time first spent at the fire. No amount of human caring or charisma alone could have made those moments so special. It was the time that I'd spent earlier in the presence of Christ that made the difference. She knew it and I knew it.

Have you ever had a time like that? Have you ever experienced a personal encounter that overflows with the essence of ideal Christian fellowship—singing, crying, laughing, remembering, praying, talking about the most intimate concerns of life and death?

None of us can make that kind of experience happen without our first abiding in the fire of Christ. Ringing in my ears as I drove home after the encounter in the hospital were his words: "Without me you can do nothing" and "with me all things are possible."

How often have I gone to the hospital, breathing life-giving promises to others without first finding his strengthening for myself! On those occasions I experienced a sense of dryness or inadequacy upon leaving. I am reminded of the wasps in New Hampshire during the late fall. They are alive, but no one fears or respects them because they are impotent and lazy. The cooling weather has done its work on them. But when the warm spring weather comes, watch out! Their strength is renewed. Then everyone pays close attention to where the wasps are and what they're doing.

Do people have to reckon with the power of God in me or am I like a wasp in the fall—barely alive and struggling in my own strength? Fire time has made the difference.

Two themes of meditation have often dominated my time at the fire with Christ. I first discovered them in a rather negative context, in Romans, chapter one, where the Apostle Paul wrote that those who were resisting certain themes were enlarging the distance between themselves and God. The first theme is that of *honoring God*.

Paul had warned that the first step downward in spiritual rebellion was the choice not to honor God. Carefully reading the beginning of many of Paul's letters will force us to see how honoring God was primary in all of his thinking. Giving God his rightful place keeps people in their rightful place.

The act of honoring God acknowledges who he is, what he has done, and what he controls. One cannot come to the fire of Christ and stay there if one is unwilling to honor him. Those who refused to honor Christ during his earthly ministry usually left his presence quickly, angrily, or sadly. Learning to honor God must become one of the inner disciplines in our lives. It's a spiritual habit slowly acquired, but a necessary one if we are to keep spiritually fresh.

Honoring God can become a spiritual discipline if it's done first at the fire with Christ. Begin to look throughout the hours of the day for things which display the beauty and the splendor of God's work. Recently I read about Joseph Priestley, an English clergyman and scientist who lived 250 years ago. He was the first person to discover that plants are "chemical factories" which, in effect, breathe in the carbon dioxide in the atmosphere and convert it to oxygen which human beings can then breathe. Suppose plants desired the same elements in the atmosphere that human beings need? Rather than cooperation in the scheme of nature, there would be competition. I guess it's no profound thing, but pausing and honoring God for the genius of his creation and then thanking him for its beautiful complexity and balance was a special moment for me.

I also find myself delighting in the various flavors God has created for our enjoyment. We honor him, I believe, when we mix flavors, aromas, and colors in cooking to produce new tastes, fragrances, and eye-appealing combinations. Even the cooking of a meal can become an offering to God, a show of honor for what he's done in revealing part of his glory to us.

A man in our present congregation is the president of a camera club that sponsors an annual international competition for amateur photographers. One year he gave our family a special showing of the best slides submitted. We sat alternately laughing and gasping at the incredibly beautiful and odd insects, birds, and animals in nature. Over and over again we were compelled to remark about our Creator God who has combined colors and shapes in ways that defy the imagination.

The root of Moses' greatness was his awareness of the glory of God. He had a continuing drive to honor him. His song on the shore of the Red Sea in Exodus 15 is full of themes that describe and honor Jehovah: strength, salvation, power, majesty, holiness, wonder-working might, leadership, love, everlasting rule. Moses knew God and was never hesitant to recite the mighty acts and attributes of the God he'd first met at the burning bush. And that is why Moses was always bold, fresh, and authoritative.

A number of years ago we dug a well in New Hampshire. As we watched the skilled men who searched for water, I thought of the proverb:

> It is the glory of God to conceal things, but the glory of kings to search things out. (Proverbs 25:2, TLB)

For those men, drilling for water was a job. For me, how-ever, a "deeper" lesson was being uncovered as I watched.

Many of King David's psalms have an interesting rhythm. David often began his writing in despair. His eyes were first on himself and his enemies. Then as David began to think through the situation, he made a deliberate choice to honor God. And when he did, the psalm abruptly shifted, always ending in triumph.

Having observed women who have sunk into unhappi-ness makes me wonder whether they haven't lost the ability to honor the God of their ministry. Worship has been re-placed by self-pity, regret, and bitterness. The result is a loss of perspective on what God is doing in people and in the world. Usually their predicament is the result of not having taken enough time to honor God.

When such attitudes prevail, conversations with other Christians are often insipid, majoring on the trivial. People therefore begin to leave one another empty of spirit. During such dry spells there is the danger of shifting our honor from God to an inordinate honoring of men. Both trivial talk and people-exalting talk ought to signal the need to exalt God.

Returning to the Apostle Paul and Romans 1, we find that in addition to the concept of honoring, Paul said that an absence of thankfulness was a second step downward in spiritual rebellion. It's also the second theme I have learned at the fire.

Paul was fond of reminding young Christians about the importance of constantly giving thanks both to God and to one another. It took Gordon and me years to discover why. We found part of the answer among older people in our circle of relationships.

Older people who are thankful are a delight to know. From talking with them, we began to learn that thankful-ness, like honoring, didn't simply happen. It was a part of a spiritual discipline which, for most of these elderly people, had begun early in their experience with Christ at the fire.

We learned from them that a consistent daily exercise of thankfulness to the Lord was an aspect of healthy Christian growth. For each individual we spoke with, it was deliberate and lifelong.

A friend in her eighties sat next to me during a speech on the effective use of time. Afterwards she turned to me and verbally thanked the Lord that she was well enough to be there. That lecture will have significance in her future. She has what I call "expectant thankfulness."

When my husband's book, *Magnificent Marriage,* was first published, we received a letter from Lee Whiston, the author of *Are You Fun to Live With?* Lee, in his eighties, wrote: "I want to thank you and the Lord for *Magnificent Marriage.* It has freed me up in my relationship to my wife."

Each time we are thankful to God, we are acknowledging our dependence upon him. We are saying, "I need you; I couldn't have done that without you." A thankful heart can never be a conceited heart; there is no room for pride in a heart which majors on thanks.

Jesus constantly expressed thanks to the Father. At the grave of Lazarus, Jesus prayed:

> *Father, I thank thee that thou hast heard me.* (John 11:41, KJV)

Again at the breaking of the bread and during his Gethsemane prayer, thanks was a major theme. Both times Jesus was reaffirming that he could do nothing without his heavenly Father.

If thankfulness is a habit we need to acquire, then how do we go about acquiring it? One day in my Sunday school class someone suggested that if the Israelites needed to annually remember their deliverance from Egypt, then perhaps we need to remember certain things also. A major aspect of the feasts and the festivals which the Israelites maintained year after year centered on appreciation and thanksgiving to God. Perhaps we ought to celebrate a personal thanksgiving day each year, taking an inventory of newly gained insights, graces, gifts, relationships, and opportunities.

The Apostle Paul reminds us that it is the will of God for us to be thankful in all things. In the MacDonald home you might frequently hear our children ask these questions: "Are you thankful?" or "Did you thank the Lord for what happened?" We've tried to get them to appreciate the priority of such questions. Now that they're getting into their older teen years, they've turned the tables on us and often ask us during difficult situations, "Are you thankful?" That's a case of the discipled edifying and encouraging the disciplers!

Being thankful for some events takes nothing less than supernatural perspective and strength. Such an attitude is born in the heart that believes every situation can be turned to our good if we will but learn to praise God in the middle of it.

Billy Bray, a Cornish coal miner, was a powerful preacher for Christ. A crotchety Christian once asked him, "What would you do if God were to shut you up in a barrel?" Billy Bray simply smiled and responded, "I'd shout glory through the bunghole." That sort of initiative is not natural. Rather, it is a grace found at a fire, the fire of Christ.

I see that same kind of resolve in the heart of a poem written by Ruth Graham, the wife of the famous evangelist:

> *Dear God,*
> *Let me soar in the face of the wind;*
> *up*
> *up*
> *like the lark,*
> *so poised and so sure,*
> *through the cold on the storm*
> *with wings to endure.*

Let the silver rain wash
all the dust from my wings,
let me soar
as he soars,
let me sing
as he sings;
let it lift me
all joyous
and carefree
and swift,
let it buffet
and drive me,
but God,
let it lift! [1]

A prayer in poetic form like that could have been written only by someone with a thankful heart. In this case the thankful heart had looked into nature, seeing things which God had given, and had acknowledged their beauty and their origin.

Just as we look for things through which to honor the Lord, so too we must look for things for which to be thankful. We need to do them consciously and make them a part of the pattern of our lives.

When I wear my gardening clothes at our New Hampshire retreat, which we call "Peace Ledge," I often find myself doing a good deal of soil testing because the rocky New England soil is so poor. The first thing I test for is acidity—is there too much of it or too little? If the soil is too acidic, or sour, then nothing grows well; if it is too alkaline, or bitter, then nothing grows well either. Both extremes are bad for most of the vegetables I might choose to grow. I have to sweeten the soil when the acid is high.

If I were doing a soil test on my spirit, thankfulness and honoring would be the two tests I'd do first. They are basic to a healthy spirit for they make growth possible.

No wonder the prophet Jeremiah wrote:

> Listen, O foolish, senseless people—you with the eyes that
> do not see and the ears that do not listen—have you no
> respect at all for me? the Lord God asks. How can it be that
> you don't even tremble in my presence? I set the shorelines
> of the world by perpetual decrees, so that the oceans, though
> they toss and roar, can never pass those bounds. Isn't such
> a God to be feared and worshiped?
>
> But my people have rebellious hearts; they have turned
> against me and gone off into idolatry. Though I am the one
> who gives them rain each year in spring and fall and sends
> the harvest times, yet they have no respect or fear for me.
> And so I have taken away these wondrous blessings from
> them. This sin has robbed them of all these good things.
> (Jeremiah 5:21-25, TLB)

That kind of rebellion did not happen overnight. A
destructive cycle is represented here. The heart that chooses
to neither honor nor thank God becomes rebellious, and the
rebellion engenders a further lack of honoring and of
thanking. Like the plant that is in soil which is too bitter or
too sour, rebellion may not be apparent to the naked eye for
some time. However, when it is, treatment must be immediate and consistent if health is to be restored.

One evening I stood applauding along with a large audience at the end of a Ken Medema concert. Ken Medema,
who is the gifted Christian singer, pianist, and composer
without eyesight, stood slowly, raised his hands toward
heaven, and began to applaud God. In so doing, he forced
the focus of the audience back to where it should be. Ironically, Ken Medema "saw" what we could not see at first:
That behind the beauty of the music is the God of gifts and
sounds and that he is the one who should be receiving our
worship and thanksgiving.

In the spring it's important to aerate the lawn if we expect healthy grass. An aerator works the hardened ground to let in air, moisture, and any nutrients we wish to add to the soil. In a similar way the inner spirit must be tested and aerated as we deliberately set out each day to find ways to thank and honor the God who has made us and called us to his son's fire.

Brigid Herman, the wife of a European pastor at the turn of the century, wrote:

> When we read the lives of the saints, we are struck by a certain large leisure which went hand in hand with a remarkable effectiveness. They were never hurried; they did comparatively few things, and these not necessarily striking or important; and they troubled very little about their influence. Yet they always seemed to hit the mark; every bit of their life told; their simplest actions had a distinction, an exquisiteness which suggested the artist. The reason is not far to seek. Their sainthood lay in their habit of referring the smallest actions to God. They lived in God; they acted from a pure motive of love toward God. They were as free from self-regard as from slavery to the good opinion of others. God saw and God rewarded; what else needed they? They possessed God and themselves in God. Hence the inalienable dignity of these meek, quiet figures that seem to produce such marvelous effects with such humble materials.[2]

The woman who told me that I would learn to hate the ministry knew nothing of the functions of disengagement at the fire. I doubt whether her life had made much room for either honoring or thanking God. As a result sourness and bitterness had set in. In looking back, I now realize that she must not have been a person who grew or caused others to grow. The qualities of honoring and thanking God must be part of a person who chooses to live in the fishbowl and wants to be useful and to experience the rewards of God. And that, in part, is why the trek to the inner fire becomes a larger and larger preoccupation on the horizon of my own life.

4
Open Hands—Unclenched Fists

You can receive nothing with drooping hands or clenched fists.
Helmut Thielicke

IT SEEMS only yesterday when Gordon and I were on the verge of entering the pastoral ministry. I retain vivid memories of the feelings that bubbled within me in those days when as a young wife I wondered what God might have in our future. A part of me anticipated the opportunity of going places, knowing people, and accomplishing great things for God. Both of us lived with a slight impatience as we anticipated the day when Gordon would finish his education and we could get on to those wonderful things we sensed were ahead.

One aspect of my inner self, however, was often in a state of agitation. While I was indeed eager to get down to the business of serving God, I could already sense the approaching pressure of a myriad of circumstances which would drain strength, threaten the health of our primary relationships, and probably expose personal inadequacies. Thus in quiet moments a sense of genuine uneasiness rippled through my spirit.

Because I clearly recall those opposing feelings and conflicting thoughts, I am always quite sympathetic to young women who visit me and reveal a similar sense of "diminished capability." As we talk, I often find myself working hard to help them see the importance of self-understanding, a key factor in the pursuit of effective ministry for any man or woman. It means that we comprehend both the strong and weak points of potential performance. The weak points are those aspects of personhood which remain immature, ultra-sensitive, or just plain dominated by the power of sin. That pursuit of self-understanding has been a very important part in the formation of my own life as the wife of a pastor.

Frankly, my view of my self has not always been a healthy one. As a teenager I remember the strong surges of inner frustration over unending battles with pimples, embarrassment over what I deemed an unsightly nose and a front tooth which should have received dental correction but didn't. As a result of my sensitivity, I often felt uneasy in crowds. I was certain that the facial blemishes, the nose, and the tooth were all that anyone ever noticed about me. As you can imagine, such a personal suspicion in the life of a teenager does nothing to engender healthy self-confidence.

It was no easy task, and it did not happen quickly, but I was able to overcome those feelings when, as a Christian woman, I realized that people could be drawn to the quality of my spirit rather than to the shape of my face. I began to see that the power which can burst from the inner person of one who chooses to be like Christ can more than compensate for any sense of personal unattractiveness that one might have. It now seems so obvious, but that discovery brought about a total change in my self-image and in terms of my worth to God and anyone else who entered the perimeter of my world.

My self-understanding began to develop as I repeatedly meditated upon biblical statements such as:

> The Lord is my light and my salvation; whom shall I fear?
> The Lord is the stronghold of my life; of whom shall I be
> afraid? (Psalm 27:1)

At times I considered the words of Paul (who apparently was not much to look at either):

> *I can do all things through Christ which strengtheneth me.* (Philippians 4:13, KJV)

When I saw how people in weakened conditions or in adverse circumstances had drawn from the strength of God, I determined that I would do likewise.

It worked! Yes, it was a long process, but it worked. I finally came to realize that I was truly God's daughter. If God were true to his Word, then I could assume that having made me, he really did love me and that he had a special usefulness for my life. I had only to discover the implications, and the direction, of that usefulness.

My "self-image" began to change dramatically. I still think my nose is too big, and I occasionally have to cover up a pimple. The tooth in the front of my mouth still crosses its neighbor just a bit, but I hardly care. I've attempted to enhance "beauty" from another source. As I've permitted that beauty to burst out of me, I've discovered a corresponding decline in those originally paralyzing feelings of inadequacy.

How did all of this happen? Looking back, I notice at least three things I did to hasten the process of self-understanding and acceptance. First, I chose to *consciously cooperate with God's love.* Then second, I chose to *risk spiritual growth even when it hurt.* And third, I determined to *discover and use the "gifts" God had given me for the good of others.*

Those three steps are not in the past tense of my life. I'm still choosing to do them on virtually a daily basis. They are a sort of personal creed, coloring all aspects of my being. Let me explain their meaning and implications a bit more.

A woman makes an enormous leap forward in her spiritual development when she determines that being *useful* is more important than being *noticed.* I am appalled at how often our culture urges us to place priority attention on our physical appearance. We thus become mindful of the things which are evaluated in terms of size and shape. And listening to this "cultural mandate," we can be tempted to try to become very beautiful—and useless.

I think of a woman I once knew whose major value to herself and to her husband was her physical beauty. He'd paid enormous sums of money to cap her teeth, fix her hair, and clothe her body so that she would be stunningly attractive to men with whom her husband wished to do business. But apart from the fact that she was good for drawing business contacts to her husband, she felt utterly useless. Ultimately their marriage ended in divorce.

If there is a beginning point in spiritual development, it is the choice one makes to become useful to God and, therefore, to others. I have a right to make this choice because I begin with the assumption that having been made by God, I am alive for a purpose. My husband often tells people that somewhere within us there must be a place on which the words "Made in heaven by God" are stamped. I am also mindful of a tiny plaque sent to me by a dear friend who knew I was hurting one day. It read: *You are beautiful! Remember, God don't make no junk!*

Cooperating with God's love means *accepting the fact that as God's product, I have a purpose and that his love makes me a special person.* Embracing that reality frees me to search for the gifts, the potential, and the insights which he has hidden within me to discover. But only when I've accepted what I'll call "creation love," can I set out to discover the meaning of my usefulness.

Some women suffer greatly from poor self-images and thus withdraw from others and grow inward, perhaps bitter and envious of others who seem to minister so easily. Others will attempt to compensate for inadequacies by trying to become something other than what they really are. They will project, for example, a highly sensual image; they may also become almost an automated robot of hard work either in the home or out on some job. Still others will compensate by slavishly tying themselves to a relationship in which all of their personhood is at stake. Those reactions come from persons who really haven't spent much time asking the big question, "What has God made *me* for?"

What I'm describing may need to be a matter of conscious, daily meditation. Many of us may have to stop and spend time each morning reminding ourselves in the presence of God that he is the one who has made us (creation love) and that he is the one who is shaping us (maturing love). On the basis of that daily reaffirmation, we can set forth to see what God is going to reveal in the coming hours to make us more useful to him and to others. Encountering such a process can be very exciting!

Some years ago on a visit to the country of Haiti, I was taken to a pottery center where a potter sat at a large wheel shaping and spinning clay into bowls and pitchers. I was impressed that the potter could apply his genius to the creation of an object of art only after the people who supplied the clay had done their job. It was their responsibility to procure the clay from the clay pits, work it with their feet until it was pliable, and then present it to the potter.

On the day of my visit, a squabble had broken out among the clay suppliers. That meant that the quantity of clay arriving at the wheel had begun to dwindle, and the quality of the clay delivered had become very poor. The result? The potter couldn't produce at the level of his capacity. As you can imagine, morale quickly went downhill.

The growing frustration of the Haitian workers absorbed me. Then suddenly I recalled that the prophet Jeremiah had reminded the people that all of us are like clay and that unavailable clay denies the potter a chance to produce useful things.

I saw in those moments the vivid meaning of the *principle of availability*. The faithfulness of unified workers who find the clay, the pliability of the clay itself, and the genius of the potter, all have to be in harmony before an object of beauty or utility can be produced.

And that process must go on and on.

The pursuit of usefulness is an everyday acknowledgment that I must, first of all, be ready for the hand of the Divine Potter to continue his "beautifying" work in my life. Or to put it another way, I must reaffirm before God that I am ready for the ways in which he is going to shape me through the circumstances and the opportunities of the hours ahead.

Helmut Thielicke once wrote, "You can receive nothing with drooping hands or clenched fists." I think he's right. It is impossible to receive anything when fists are clenched and hands are drooping. Submitting to the Divine Potter is like putting one's hands out, opening one's fists, and saying, "Lord, today I choose to cooperate with your maturing love. Make me more beautiful—like Christ today."

In the words of E. Stanley Jones, accepting maturing love means that we will "bear nothing and use everything." I'm impressed with the number of examples of that principle in Scripture. Jesus Christ *used* the unexpected intrusion of 5,000 people upon his rest time to teach the disciples compassion. He *used* the interruption by Zacchaeus, the little man in the tree, as an occasion to change a man's life and to demonstrate to a community the meaning of repentance. The Apostle Paul *used* prison time for worship, for evangelism, for teaching, and for writing to young congregations that he'd previously established. Biblical men and women of God never saw any circumstance as pointless.

Was a day recently spent in my garden a waste of time? Looking at my journal entry for that day, I find that that gardening time was useful for hearing something special from the Lord:

> Removing the spent blossoms on petunias is essential to new blossoms. Today as I removed the old, I was reminded of how essential it is to my life to enjoy each blossom in my life, but to remember to pull it off

when spent and move on to new experiences. Many live trying to keep memories of dead blossoms alive only to miss the potential of the new and present bloom.

I strongly feel that God spoke to me that day in the garden. I needed only to listen to discern his message. Pressing meaning into the smallest duties and happenings has given added color to my life. Experiences which might otherwise have seemed mundane or worthy of ignoring have come alive.

Another day of "duty" brought this journal entry:

Harvest, how I love it! Apples, tomatoes, cukes, and enough zucchini to share with the block. Wait till the family sees! I processed the apples and placed them in the Foley food mill. As I watched it separate the useful from the waste, my thoughts meandered to my life and God's "Foley food mill" process on me. Conversations of the past week came to my mind and I had to ask myself which would have come out on the useful side and which would be waste.

Lord, use your purging on me and remove those attitudes and actions which are unnecessary or not pleasing to you, multiplying what shows your goodness.

The resolve to accept and to use everything enabled General William Booth, founder of the Salvation Army, to accept even blindness. His response was:

God knows best. I have done what I could for Him and people with my eyes. Now I shall do what I can for God and the people without my eyes.[1]

I think cooperating with God's maturing love also means *consciously walking away from sin*. I say that because I don't think that many Christian women hate sin enough. I believe that one of the major roles God's Spirit plays in our lives is to signal us when an attitude or an act is out of line with God's expected level of performance for us. In a sense, God holds each of us to a level of behavior proportionate to our insight, our experience, our blessing. To whatever point that is, the Holy Spirit is alert to prod us during moments of belligerence.

Sin for me may be an unkind thought when the phone rings—again. It might be a poor, self-pitying attitude if my husband has one too many meetings in a week or a lack of forgiveness when I've been misunderstood or transmitting "information" which is actually gossip. I must learn to hate those things and turn my strength against them.

If removing pimples from my face and straightening out my teeth are ways to help me achieve physical attractiveness, then spiritual beauty can come only as the blemishes of the spirit are treated by God's love—his maturing love with which I must cooperate.

Cooperating with God's love also means *learning from failures and falls.* My life is a chain of failures from which I've learned the most valuable lessons. I would never have desired even one of those failures, but having failed, I count the resulting lessons priceless.

How important it is not to be paralyzed by failure! The secret is to be teachable in vulnerable moments of failure and go on. Proverbs says that the righteous man may fall seven times but gets up again. Jonah's great comfort to us is that God gave him a second chance:

> *Then the word of the Lord came to Jonah a second time.* (Jonah 3:1)

Christ anticipated failure in Peter long before Peter failed, but Christ also had a tomorrow for Peter and comforted him *ahead of time:*

But I have pleaded in prayer for you that your faith should not completely fail. So when you have repented and turned to me again, strengthen and build up the faith of your brothers. (Luke 22:32, TLB)

David reminds us that God loves us as a father loves his children:

For he knows that we are but dust. . . . (Psalm 103:14, TLB)

The suggestion is that God expects the common failures and blunders which are typical of growing children. My husband and I expect our fifteen-year-old to behave like a fifteen-year-old. We don't consider her a failure for not being like a twenty-year-old.

The fact is that many of us are like people in the Scriptures: Jonah, Moses, David, Peter, John Mark, and a host of others whose lives were marked by not only great performances, but also great failures. And their failures rewarded them with insights and opportunities for new starts in the grace of God. From their failures they grew into spiritual giants.

Last year a new food store opened in our community. I went early the first day and was overwhelmed by the friendliness of the store personnel. It put me in such a frame of mind that I soon bought twice as much as I had planned! Later driving home, I thought about my experience in that store. My reflections were captured in my journal:

The store reminded me of the freshness of each new spring and summer—new starts in Christian experience. Knowing that each day can be "opening day" in my walk with Christ is so comforting. It was more then groceries being bought. It was a cheer to new starts. Oh, some filled their baskets and left but I grew.

Cooperating with God's maturing love may also mean *surrendering any anger we may have hidden in our hearts*. At Peace Ledge, our retreat in New Hampshire, there is an old, abandoned well which was dug by farmers long ago. Down deep is a pool of water which the state of New Hampshire says is polluted and undrinkable. It reminds me of the pools of anger that can often sit deep, polluted, and ugly within our innermost being. One day when someone least expects it, the anger may explode in an unguarded moment from within our hidden reservoir and hurt another. We'll become embarrassed and the heart of God will be wounded.

Anger has been a hard thing for me. In ministry one is often exposed to a lot of sin. It's easy for me to get angry with myself or with people who act sinfully toward others. Frequently what draws anger from me is seeing others do what I dislike in myself—the psychologists call that reaction "projection."

God's maturing love calls us to deal with our anger in a holy way. Like Joseph who had reason to be angry with his brothers, we must choose to look upon hurtful moments in life as times when God can make us beautiful—like Christ. Joseph told his brothers,

> *You meant evil against me; but God meant it for good . . . that people should be kept alive. . . .* (Genesis 50:20)

I began to conquer anger as a force within me when I realized that most of us do not actually mean to hurt others. Jesus prayed on the cross:

> *Father, forgive them; for they know not what they do.* (Luke 23:34)

The disciples hadn't meant to hurt Jesus when they slept through his darkest hours. He was hurt but certainly not angry. He protected them when they ran away as his captors approached. And he didn't rail at them when they later met after his resurrection. Anger would have destroyed men of God in the making.

Accepting the fact that *angry people cannot grow* and become useful, I have repeatedly asked God to uncover those dark pools lying beneath the surface of my consciousness. I've prayed the same on behalf of others. Where he has revealed my own pockets of anger to me, I've tried hard to face them and give them to him for resolution. The release has been tremendous.

Cooperating with God's maturing love also means *treating my body correctly*. I'm impressed with the words of Paul as he concludes his letter to the Thessalonians:

> May the God of peace himself sanctify you wholly; and may your spirit and soul and body be kept sound and blameless at the coming of our Lord Jesus Christ. (1 Thessalonians 5:23)

Women are always aware of their bodies. Changes within our hormonal balances are always sending us signals that can affect moods, strength levels, and even our perceptual capacities. If we don't understand those things, thinking positively about them and accepting them, our bodies can betray us and leave us in a nongrowth predicament.

A fellow-learner in a class I taught shared thoughts about the tendency of many women to fight depression in the fall of the year. She reminded us that Psalm 1 suggests that we are all to be like trees planted by a stream—trees which bear fruit "in . . . season."

Her insight? That even trees don't flower and bear fruit all the time—only in season. But men and women alike seem to think that we should be bearing fruit all the time; we punish ourselves when we're not. She was teaching us the beauty of personal dormancy: We must allow for it and accept it joyfully.

I realize that the earlier years when Gordon and I were full of extra vitality were a growing period during which we had to gather strength and maturity for the fruit-bearing years. If we'd been allowed to do everything in the first years of our lives together, we would have soon exhausted our strength in the pursuit of things for which we lacked wisdom and experience. And now years later at some of the peak strides of our lives and ministry, we've learned that it remains unwise not to withdraw and find seasons of spiritual and relational dormancy.

What is dormancy? A time of inner strength-gathering for a better bloom later. If there is no dormancy, there will be no bloom. That holds true both in the life of trees and in the life of people who have been given the privilege of spiritual leadership.

Another one of my journal entries reads:

> Fall 1980 had to break all records for beauty. Soon the trees will be bare and look dead, but they are far from dead. They are gathering strength for the big bud of the spring of '81. Their outward appearance is quite deceiving. Some of my deepest learning times have come when it seemed that I was fruitless too. May I learn not to duck the dormant periods.

Most of us women have had very dependable bodies. Some of us must frankly accept the fact that we're "on the shelf" for a day or two each month. That is not a license for complete withdrawal, but it is instead a recognition that we often need to pace ourselves and learn that some days have to be different in terms of expectational levels and output.

Again my journal has been extremely helpful in allowing me to chart the cycles of my year. Its record of my past has helped me to understand under what conditions and at what times I can expect more or less of myself. It has also helped me to remember when other people will tend to be hurting very badly and may need me (or others like me) to be a strong right arm in their lives.

As the principle of dormancy suggests the need for withdrawal in which to gain strength to bloom, let me add a corollary related to cooperating with God's maturing love: the need for also *accepting the "downtimes"* of my life. Our family calls them "Elijah moments," and they come after great outpourings of energy. Both my husband and I have come to accept a certain amount of low-level depression after a hard weekend, a major thrust in ministry, or a lot of people-involved ministry. To be spiritually, mentally, and emotionally exhausted is no disaster. Neither is it an indication of our failure to grow or mature.

All of us in leadership simply have to come to grips with the fact that there are going to be moments when the mind and the spirit are spent and need maximum relaxation. It is hard work to sense what people need when you're among them. Listening to the hidden agendas that spin out of conversations can be exhausting. In general, spiritual battles are draining. That's a fact which Gordon and I have had to face, and so we've learned to accept the downtimes, realizing that during those moments, we must neither make big decisions nor formulate value judgments about ourselves or anyone else. It's important that we back off for a day and do simple things. The angel of the Lord told Elijah:

Arise and eat, else the journey be too great for you. (1 Kings 19:7)

In other words, "Elijah, do the simple and necessary thing."

Downtimes can be very valuable, for God may allow us to get a more accurate picture of those aspects of our lives which may have become distorted due to pride of achievement or success. The end result of such clearer vision may be greater self-awareness and sense of perspective as we recover our emotional and mental strength.

I've been helped by meditating on various psalms. In Psalm 42, for example, I hear David talking *to* his mood, rather than letting his mood talk or dictate to him. He reminds himself of better days ahead, recalling the good days of the past—even if the present is the "pits." Spending a few hours reading light literature, listening to pleasant music, playing ball with the children, or even writing in my personal journal have all been helpful. During the down-times the temptation to self-pity is particularly strong and one to guard against carefully!

I think about those things when a young woman visits me and observes that she is not capable of the pressure cooker life of ministry. And I suppose I think the same thoughts when I observe men or women who think that they've gotten it all put together even before they've had a chance to get into the heart of things. In both cases, what will lift one person and level another is the work of God's maturing love.

When the Father in heaven is allowed to shape the clay of our lives in the vulnerable moments, products of increasing beauty will appear. Christ's attractiveness will burst forth and many will be moved to honor God.

A few years ago a small boy in our congregation came up at the end of a service, fixed a perplexing stare upon me, and finally said quite seriously, "Mrs. Mac, is your front tooth falling out?" I suspect that he wanted to commiserate with me because he was in a phase when his own front teeth were indeed falling out. Rather than let myself be destroyed by diminished self-confidence, I was destroyed by laughter.

After explaining my dental predicament to my young friend, I found myself walking away, delighted that the center of what beauty I am trying to pursue is not in my mouth but in my heart.

5
The Further Pursuit of Beauty

*God has purposes concerning us which He has not yet unfolded;
therefore, each day grows sacred in wondering expectation.*
Phillips Brooks

THE magazine advertisement features the photo of an attractive model with an enviable growth of blond hair. It suggests that beauty is found in a bottle of hair conditioner. Perhaps there is some truth to the ad if you and I assume that beauty is a quality to be noticed and admired.

What woman doesn't desire the beauty that makes people notice and admire her? Count me among them as I daily pursue a regimen of physical attractiveness that will delight my husband and draw him to me. However, the beauty which arouses only notice and admiration is temporary and certainly insufficient. It must not be taken out of proportion and pursued at the expense of a more mature beauty.

The beauty I've discovered to be far more important is the beauty which reflects the living Christ and his power to make people whole human beings. And, as I've already said, that insight opened the way to a new awareness of who I am as a person and what God is making me to be. I began to understand it when I chose to cooperate with the maturing love of God.

But there are further steps in the pursuit of wholeness that can make us women capable of living with leadership responsibility and privilege. In the passing years my attention has been drawn to the principle of growth and the fact that it is both natural *and* painful.

Everyone likes the fruits of personal development; few appreciate the pains of the process. But growth of the right kind hurts at times. We have to breathe deeply and dive into growth, trusting that God, the Divine Potter with whom we have chosen to cooperate, knows what he is doing. That's what's behind my second principle of becoming adequate to the challenges of ministry: *Risk growth even if it hurts.*

Somewhere I read of a country road sign which said:

> Be careful which rut you choose. You will be in it for the next 25 miles.

Anyone who lives in a rut understands the meaning of boredom. Whether one drives in a rut or lives in one, the point is that there is no need to worry about the direction in which one is moving. The rut will do all the steering that is needed. But to get out of the rut means that one must make some hard choices about a sense of direction and a level of personal being—and that spells growth.

All healthy life reflects growth, part of which means trying to avoid a lifelong rut. Let's be very sure to understand that. "Rutless living" means risk, potential failure, and a lot of personal decisions. It means hard work, discipline, and perseverance. While it suggests a certain amount of suffering, it also adds up to health!

After having spent a great deal of time with women, I can more easily spot those who are growing and those who have settled for the status quo. Where a growing woman is a leader, the people following her will tend to grow. Conversely, if she is not growing, then the followers will also stagnate or else move to another leader.

Let me paint my thoughts on growth with some broad strokes. While my notion of growth is very practical and down-to-earth, I also believe that the theme of growth has to spread to all dimensions of life. We have to step out into new areas of experimentation and expression even if we fail or are outdone by someone else.

What does growth mean? Take intellectual growth, for example. There is no excuse for any of us not to have our minds bent toward the acquisition of knowledge. Gerhardt Tersteegen (1649–1700) said:

> Make room for everything which is capable of rejoicing, enlarging, or calming the heart. . . .[1]

Many years ago God began challenging me to keep my mind sharpened and expanding—a challenge I might have neglected as the mother of small children with whom I talked only baby talk. I was fortunate enough to sense that that was a vulnerable period of time in our family, for my husband could have slowly drawn away from me as his mind grew and mine stagnated. I made a conscious choice not to let those things happen and they didn't.

I followed certain reading disciplines. That was something I had to work on because in those days manual things always seemed to scream more loudly for my attention than mental tasks. But I will always be grateful for the growing love I developed for devouring the printed page.

One doesn't have to be a scholar to read; all it takes is a small amount of time set aside each day for becoming acquainted with one book a week. Few books are really worth reading completely through, but a basic knowledge both of what various authors are saying and of how to retrieve that material later on is quite important. I've learned to keep a notebook in which to record the insights of authors and new titles others recommend to me. Among the most enjoyable moments of our marriage are those times when Gordon and I exchange discoveries from our reading and trade quotes that will be useful in the formation of a talk or a new manuscript.

Growth can occur in other dimensions of life. It happens, for example, when you or I determine to learn a new craft each year. While it isn't necessary to master the art of decoupage or flower arranging or furniture refinishing, it certainly enhances our sense of discovery to understand what's involved and then attempt to engage in new tasks to whatever level of mastery we can attain. I think that is close to what Edith Schaeffer means when she challenges her readers to condition the "creative muscles" lest they atrophy.

A long time ago I decided to make gifts which Gordon and I could give to people as symbols of affection or appreciation. I discovered a thousand things that any of us can make. And making those things has provided me with another dimension of growth. More than once I've asked my husband to drive a bit slower on the way to dinner at a friend's home. My requests didn't come because he was speeding and a radar trap was down the road, but rather because I was still sewing a hand towel which could be looped through a cabinet handle in someone's kitchen or completing the crocheting of a toilet paper cover for that extra roll in someone's bathroom.

Someday my children will look back at my yearly calendars and recall that whenever I accepted an invitation to dinner from someone on the phone, I ended the conversation by asking the colors of her bathroom or kitchen. The answers were carefully noted on the calendar space. An entry might read: 6:30 P.M., Friday, casual clothes, lime green. That last piece of data, referring to the hostess' color scheme, would guide me in making something suitable.

Gifts need not be extravagant to be meaningful, I've found. When I give a baby gift, I also give the other siblings three crisp one-dollar bills along with a note of thanks for their helping their parents and a suggestion that they take their parents out for ice cream. Needless to say, the siblings are "strangely warmed" that their pastor and his wife would think of them in such a personal way. And the parents are thrilled that the need of their older child or children for recognition has been noted. At a time of abundant gifts to the newborn, the siblings can easily feel left out. The gift of ice-cream money from Gordon and me has thus served to compensate for that empty feeling!

Finding ways to give to others has had its decided reward experienced in seeing others made happy by simple tokens of love and thoughtfulness. The joy of giving has helped me become more aware of the needs of others. What are other ways of experiencing personal growth?

Personal growth also comes through the ability to ask good questions. One can easily divide people into two categories when it comes to conversation: those who ask questions and those who are always anxious to give answers. A good question draws out people's experiences, their dreams and aspirations, their hurts, and their discoveries. A knowledge of what they have to share helps me to grow and will help me to minister at a later time.

From somewhere in his childhood my husband learned both the value and the art of asking questions. I often used to watch in amazement as he would draw people out on matters of vocation, personal history, or various real-life struggles and pressures. Through the use of well-placed questions, he could draw out insights which not only helped him to minister to them, but also added to a growing reservoir of information and understanding for his future work. Determining to copy him, I learned how to ask those same kinds of questions. That art has also worked for me.

I learned, for example, never to let a simple comment like "John and I had to go home this weekend" go by without my asking a question. A response might be "Was that a warm experience for the both of you?" It would not only show my interest, but also pave the way for further dialogue and ministry.

My desire for growth has also led me to explore the meaning of color and its effect on our home and clothing. I learned how to vary accent colors as the seasons change and to create a mood or an atmosphere that reminds my family how much I love making our home a place full of pleasant surprises. I can never go through a New England autumn without being newly inspired to ponder God's interest in color. Nothing reminds me more of God's glory than that tremendous display of color! It also stimulates me to make my home reflect some of that same glory.

Obviously, nature and my association with it have been great opportunities for personal growth. I've learned that growth is possible through the experiences in my garden. My mind is constantly bubbling with insights or illustrations as I handle the stuff of nature and again see how God has penetrated his creation with all sorts of spiritual parallels, as one of my recent journal entries illustrates:

> I laughed out loud at myself. No one was there, so it didn't matter. For much of the summer I have been systematically removing spider webs from my flower boxes each time we come up to Peace Ledge. But today as I viewed the massive, well-developed webs, I finally said to myself, "The web isn't your problem, Gail. Go for the spider." How typical of us mortals. We pull away the symptoms week after week without going to the root cause and dealing with it. Sorry, spider. Doomsday is here.

One can make a growth experience even out of a simple act like walking in the late afternoon. A co-worker of mine has developed a Bible study this year; part of her emphasis has been to highlight the great amount of walking that our Lord did. Her study has challenged each of us to imagine the things the Lord might have observed in nature and in people had he walked along our path. She also frequently asks us to think about how he might have reacted had he seen the same things we see. Her insight has already opened many areas of discovery for me. As Gordon and I take our frequent late afternoon walks, we fix our eyes upon the smallest details of nature around us. What we have learned has stimulated both our minds and our overall growth experience.

You can see yourself in nature if you try. Thanks to the growing interest which my family has had in the world of birds, we've studied several of their patterns of migration, their relational temperaments, their feeding habits, and their sizes and shapes. Did you know that the male house wren is a habitual nest-starter? He stuffs any likely nesting cavity with twigs, grass, and other materials, perhaps to mark his territory and perhaps as an inducement to the females when they arrive. Moreover,

> as soon as they appear, the busy male sings to draw attention. He courts one ardently, wings quivering, tail flicking straight up. If she proves receptive, he escorts her around his prospective nest sites. The female almost always disapproves of her mate's home-building efforts. After she selects one of his sites, she usually removes all of the materials and starts the nest all over again. Sometimes she collects strange items. One nest contained 52 hairpins, 188 nails, 4 tacks, 13 staples, 10 pins, 11 safety pins, 6 paper clips, 2 hooks, 3 garter fasteners, and a buckle.[2]

I've grown through reading those words because I've identified them with something in my own life and in the lives of other people. The female house wren and her dissatisfaction with the things which are done for her are a warning and a reminder of the kind of people we need *not* be. Thank God for a study of the birds which not only enlightens our curiosity, but also helps us to grow!

Sometimes themes of interest in life can overlap, becoming not only growth stimulants to the mind, but also points of economic good sense. For example, I have always enjoyed taking broken, discarded things and trying to remake them into something useful and worthwhile.

On occasion someone will call and say that she has something like a chair with one leg missing and asks if I would like it. "Of course," I always say. And the object becomes one more part of our home's furniture, all of which is layered with "antiquing." Scrape down through the layers of many of the things in our living room and you will have an archeological report of the various periods of our pastoral and family history!

Some years ago my husband's good friend and associate, Lyle Jacobson, organized a campaign in our church to furnish the apartment of a welfare recipient, a woman who had been burned out of her home. When people volunteered pieces, he borrowed a pickup, collected the items, and brought them to the woman's apartment. She selected what she wanted, suggesting he take the rest to the dump.

It was typical of Lyle and his great sense of humor to stop by our home on the way to the dump and ask if we wanted any of the rejects. And there was indeed one old table splotched with all sorts of paint; it had apparently stood in somebody's basement for many years. Someone had obviously stored all of his old paint cans on it. Lyle stopped teasing when we surprised him, suggesting that we'd save him a trip to the dump with the table and take it for ourselves. Sometime later we stripped off all the paint and found a beautiful wood grain underneath. Of course, refinishing it took hard work and a lot of time. But the table the lady on welfare rejected has been our kitchen dining table for over ten years.

That table is just one of a number of pieces which others rejected but which we reclaimed.

A few nights ago we entertained a small group from our congregation in our living room. One of the men was sitting on a reclaimed chair which, like the kitchen table, had once been on its way to the dump. We had saved its life at the last minute, brought it home, and had it reupholstered. It is now probably the most attractive piece of furniture that we own. Gordon turned to the man sitting in that chair and told him about the chair's origin. Apparently the message was caught in both its physical and spiritual application, for later the man's wife wrote us a letter saying in part:

> The story about the chair my husband was sitting in was really apropos... and the fact that he was sitting in the chair was even more perfect. He has a group of fifth-grade Sunday school boys that he has been ready to take to the dump for several weeks, but he has decided, as a result of hearing the story, to salvage each boy, to do a bit of repair work on each, and to see if they cannot be reupholstered in God's grace and turned out as handsome, as sturdy, and as useful as your chair.

I suspect that both the man and the boys grew just the way we did when we used our elbow grease to make that chair what it is today.

Of all the kinds of growth, none is more valuable or more enduring than that which occurs from investing our selves in the lives of others. If, for example, you decorated your home only for yourself, there would be dissatisfaction and resulting boredom. However, if the decoration of a home is based upon making it a place of warmth for all who enter to find love and rest, then everyone, including you the decorator, will grow and be enriched.

I must underscore the fact that the best kinds of growth are not all "fun and games." They involve taking risks in areas we consider weak or inept. We will have to risk the embarrassment of first-time failures.

We may be misunderstood, and there will certainly be occasions when we are asked questions for which we have no answers. Growth takes place when we refuse to be de-

75

fensive when our motives are questioned—when we have attempted to do something with our whole heart. In short, growth always happens when we submit to the Master Potter who has a shape for us that only he understands.

Perhaps my belief in the process of growth is best symbolized in an experience Gordon and I faced this past summer. He had been most anxious to take our canoe into the Maine wilderness for an extended camping trip. I confess that I am strictly a motel-type, and when I add the fact that I share a lot of the swimming propensities of a rock, you can understand that I swallowed several times when he asked me to go along.

Staying home would have been to choose a "rut," while going into the wilderness meant an opportunity for a new kind of growth. I went. It would be delightful to tell you that the trip progressed without a flaw. It didn't. Because of low water levels which made many portages a necessity and because of nasty weather which made for high winds and therefore difficult paddling, the trip came close to being a disaster.

On many occasions in the wilderness we could have lashed out at each other. However, both of us sensed we were testing our relationship, and we were determined to make adversity a growing experience. Frankly we would have avoided all of it had we known about the difficult weather ahead of time. Since we were already into it, we had no choice but to accept it with courage and grace. Looking back now, we share the memory of a challenge over which we can laugh. Most importantly, our lives have grown closer together because we accepted the risk and the hurts and finished the course.

Now each time I'm challenged to launch out on a new effort with no promise of success, I remember the Maine canoe trip and say to myself, "I made it then and I'll make it now." You always grow when you can look at each moment from that sort of framework, even if it hurts.

6
The Joy of Discovery

Life is an exciting business and most exciting when it is lived for others. Helen Keller

I STARTED out serving the Lord as a singer. My parents had invested large sums of money in voice lessons for me, and my earliest dreams about my own worth to God always centered on the possibility of becoming a vocal musician. I never realized how much those lessons would pay off.

My husband often tells people that he picked up his first preaching experiences on the strength of my voice. We teamed up, and people who asked me to sing were told that I sang only if Gordon was speaking. Things soon began to change when the people who'd come to hear me sing discovered that he had something worthwhile to say. I doubt if it's true, but he claims that my voice was the human key to his start as a preacher. Even if it is only half true, it makes a lovely story!

With the passage of years, however, I've discovered that voices grow old. What do you do with a talent that is fading, especially if that's the key to your sense of self-worth? If my usefulness to God and others had been seen only in terms of singing, I would be a very troubled woman today.

It's important that you understand that fact because I am convinced that the key to long-term self-worth lies in the discovery, not of talents, but rather of spiritual gifts which God has given to every person who has chosen to follow Christ. As far as I'm concerned, there's a great difference between talents and gifts. I am certainly pleased that I once developed the talent the Lord gave me, but I'm even more delighted that the spiritual gifts the Lord gives to every believer have been developed in my life also. It is my own theory that while talents may diminish with age, gifts only seem to improve and deepen with the passing of the years. That's very important, and that's why I believe that women in leadership need to work hard at discovering and developing their gifts.

Why is it that many belittle the gifts within them, forgetting that the Holy Spirit uses our faltering attempts when we are obedient and causes spiritual maturity in others?

A New Testament Christian by the name of Barnabas apparently had the gift of encouragement. What if he'd never discovered it or, having known about it, had never used it? Among the results of the utilization of Barnabas' gift were the grooming of John Mark, who wrote a very important Gospel in the New Testament, and the launching of the Apostle Paul, who began a very important teaching ministry at the church in Antioch. One could easily reason that over half the New Testament would not have been written had it not been for Barnabas' willingness to employ his gift in the lives of both John Mark and Paul.

It is no secret that Peter (1 Peter 4:10), among others, taught that everyone of us enjoys a gift that is meant to build up others in the community of faith. But while everyone may have a gift, not everyone has ever taken the time to discover what it is nor even how to develop it.

Not long ago I went browsing through a used bookstore.

As usual I succumbed to the temptation to purchase some books and found myself leaving with three biographies. The books themselves were over 100 years old. They were short so I was able to read them all rather quickly. As I did, I realized that I was the first to read them since some of the pages had remained uncut from the time of publishing. I thought about the need to split apart many of the pages and later wrote in my journal:

> Those books remind me of many people I know. So many neat things inside of us, untapped by disinterest, lying dormant—useless. Yet one of those biographies has marked my life. Too bad the original owner didn't know that there were special gifts in those books to challenge him and sold his unused books to an antique dealer.

I guess I could say that I owe the discovery and the development of my own gift of Bible teaching to my husband. He claims that he saw it in me long before I did. He lovingly pushed and chided me to say yes to teaching opportunities. While I was terribly frightened in the early days of my teaching experience, I soon grew to love what I was doing. Now I feel at home teaching the Bible and am still surprised at the ministry of the Holy Spirit in my life each time I am able to open the Scriptures before a group of women. Gifts are like that.

The discovery of a person's gift is not the same as filling slots in a church program. Sometimes in a small church the wife of a pastor or a leader must accept responsibility for doing things which are not necessarily in the area of one's gifts. But the normal situation should be that each of us works in the context of the gifts which God has developed in us. If you and I begin to show the fruits of enjoying and enhancing our gifts, others will be led to discover and enjoy theirs also.

Findley Edge, in *The Greening of the Church,* is very helpful, when he shares what it means to discover gifts. He suggests that each of us look into ourselves on the basis of three criteria: *First,* we ought to look for something called the "eureka," an I've-found-it feeling that comes when we're doing something one day that just seems to fit our temperament and style. *Second,* seek out those moments when an awareness creeps up on us that we're often dreaming dreams about serving in a particular area. Are there moments when we find that our minds are a fountain of ideas and methods about how to engage in a certain project or service? *Third,* when we find ourselves talking about certain ministries to others and we're not able to quench our own enthusiasm, we can learn something about our potential gifts.[1]

Peace Ledge, our New Hampshire retreat, was a farm that had been unused for more than thirty years. When we first took over the land a few years ago, the weeds and underbrush were in complete control. It was weeks before I discovered that hidden among those weeds were indications that things had originally been planted according to a plan. When we began to clear out the weeds, a remarkable thing appeared: We discovered a well-laid out garden with worthwhile things that wanted permission to grow. Today when people visit Peace Ledge, they are delighted with the beauty of things. And they are surprised when I show them the outlines of a plan of growth that was set in motion years ago, apparent once the undergrowth had been cleared out.

I strongly suspect that many of us are like that. We allow ourselves to be unused, and we become grown-over fields covered with weeds. Some of those weeds have particular names. There is the I-can't-do-it weed, and the I-won't-do-it weed, and the nobody-needs-me weed. Those weeds need to be taken out quickly. If the plan of God's gifts is to be uncovered in any person, a clearing process must take place. Only then will there be fulfillment and spiritual wealth.

When I look back upon the clearing process in my own

life, I discover that an interesting thing has happened to me over the years. As I came to enjoy the gift of teaching more and more, the less interested I became in developing the talent of singing. Being sensitive to this matter, I have been aware again and again of singers who are growing old and losing the edge to once beautiful voices. Rather than becoming sweeter with age, they themselves have grown more and more miserable in their attempts to serve the Lord with a talent which fewer and fewer people desire to see them perpetuate. If only they could have had a point at which they might have been open to receiving a gift.

I really believe that our gifts are discovered most quickly when our motivation is nothing more than a pure response to Christ's love. *A woman must choose to be faithful to him, not to be noticed*—one may often become blind to a talent. Jesus reminded us that one finds life by choosing to lose it in the interest of others. He said that the humble, not the proud, would be lifted up. Perhaps that's what the writer in Proverbs meant when he wrote:

He who waters others, waters himself.

Moses was concerned about that principle when he addressed the Hebrew people:

You shall not do as we are doing here today, every man pleasing himself—for you have not yet reached the resting-place and possession which the Eternal your God is to give you. (Deuteronomy 12:8, 9, Moffatt translation)

From Moses, from Jesus Christ, and from the early church, the Scripture keeps reminding us of this reality: That gifts and opportunities come to the ones committed to giving themselves away in God's service.

The women I unashamedly admire and use as models are those who view all of life through servants' eyes. They've chosen to cooperate with God's love, my first principle, and

81

thus grow and reveal beautiful gifts from which everyone profits. And they all have this in common: *They don't need to be noticed.* Theirs is a spirit of self-forgetfulness. In that humility they tend to draw crowds around them because they exude spiritual strength and power. Humility and power—how beautifully paradoxical!

I think Henrietta Mears was such a person. Some of the most effective leaders and movements of evangelical Christianity have been birthed through her influence. She may well have been among the greatest Christians of the twentieth century. I am told by those who knew her that when she entered a room, people often had the feeling that she was saying to each person, "Where have you been? I've been looking all over for you." You would never have caught her walking into a room and saying in contrast, "I'm Henrietta Mears, Miss Sunday School. Anyone want my autograph?" Her secret? Like Christ, she was always asking, "How may I serve you?"

Mary, the mother of Christ, best exemplified the model woman. She was young and must have possessed enormous inner strength. Imagine the trust she must have had in God in order to cooperate with such a miracle as the birth of Jesus. She must also have had great strength to accept the gossip, to affirm Joseph, and to keep the entire event and its origin a secret:

> *Mary kept all these things and pondered them in her heart.*
> (Luke 2:19, KJV)

I am amazed when I think of Mary's performance! She played a crucial role in presenting the Messiah to the world, but she kept quiet about it. A woman like that grows and becomes useful, though not necessarily noticed.

When Mary visited her relative, Elizabeth, the Holy Spirit moved Elizabeth to rejoice in Mary's special favor before God. Both women were free to enjoy the miracle without jealousy or haughtiness or a sense of a generation gap. They apparently found it easy to share and to care for one another. Mary cooperated with God's love by allowing Elizabeth to be God's gift of encouragement and affirmation to her. And, I might add, Elizabeth cooperated with God's love by building up Mary rather than tearing her apart through personal envy. The older served the younger; the younger was free to draw strength from the older.

You could also say that Mary was cooperative and willing to risk growth when she permitted Jesus to leave the "nest" early. Think of it: Her empty nest syndrome began when Jesus was just twelve years of age. There's just enough of a hint of anxiety in Mary's mothering life to convince me that that must not have been an easy experience for her. Yet, she cooperated, and in her acceptance of her role, Jesus found it possible to grow in wisdom and in stature.

Somewhere in Mary's life she had also made a conscious habit of saying yes to God's love. No fists clenched, no drooping hands. She said:

> I am the handmaid of the Lord; let it be to me according to your Word. (Luke 1:38)

Mary's attitudes are a powerful model for me. They tell me that a woman who cooperates with God's love, who risks growth even when it may hurt, and who seeks to be at the disposal of whatever makes others grow is going to be quite a woman.

Not all of this process is pain free or pleasurable; neither is it glamorous. I am quite careful to explain those realities to the young woman who comes to talk about her sense of inadequacy in assuming the role of a leader or a pastor's wife or whatever else God has for her. She has to accept the fact that the road of her future may indeed be paved with some failures, with some conflicts, with some disappointment, even rejection. But it isn't all that bad, and through that process God will shape her into a woman who can be a conduit of strength for other women, for her husband, and for the church of Jesus Christ. The end result is worth it all. That's the kind of beauty I can understand.

7
An Uncommon Union

A worthy wife is her husband's joy and crown; the other
kind corrodes his strength and tears down everything he does.
(Proverbs 12:4, TLB)

HISTORIANS generally agree that Jonathan Edwards was America's first great theologian. He and his wife, Sarah, lived in New England and pastored several churches over 200 years ago. While scholars have thrilled to Edwards' thought, I have found myself drawn again and again to the quality of the marriage and the family life that Jonathan and Sarah shared.

Among Jonathan Edwards' last words before he died were those of gratitude to Sarah for the "uncommon union" which they had enjoyed.[1] An uncommon union it certainly had been. Out of it had come ten children and a host of spiritual children. Young men and women, drawn to the quality of mind and spirit found in the Edwards' home, had then gone out to serve the God of Jonathan and Sarah Edwards.

One hundred and twenty-five years after the death of Edwards, between four and five hundred of their descendants gathered in Stockbridge, Massachusetts, for a family reunion and celebrated the contributions their famous ancestors had made. From them had come headmasters, poets, musicians, linguists, publishers, pastors, college presidents, doctors, and a host of people who were making positive additions to their generation. And of the marriage of Jonathan and Sarah, President Woolsey of Yale—himself a descendant—said, "Sarah had been the resting place of Jonathan's soul."

Whenever I begin to rethink the role of a woman who is wife to a man in Christian leadership, Sarah Edwards immediately assumes new importance to me. And I am refreshed by the words of Woolsey: "Sarah was a resting place for Jonathan's soul."

Hudson Taylor, the great pioneer missionary to China, also enjoyed a similar kind of relationship with his wife, Maria. A courageous man, Taylor was badly in need of a partner in life who knew how to drain off the worst that was in him and enhance the best. J. C. Pollack writes of Taylor's wife, Maria:

> Maria tempered without quenching his zeal, was largely responsible for the common sense and balance characteristic of Taylor at the height of his power. She made him take holidays. Under the influence of her less mercurial yet gay temperament he shed those moods of melancholy; he would discuss every matter with her and forget to be introspective. He became more assured, grew up; Hudson Taylor at twenty-eight, forthright as at twenty-two, no longer was on the defensive, no longer a prig. Her passionate nature fulfilled his warm-blooded yearning to love and be loved. She gave him full response, fostering and feeding affection so that together they had such a reservoir of love that it splashed over to refresh all, Chinese or European, who came near them.[2]

These two men—Edwards and Taylor—marked their generations. Because they were effective, literally tens of thousands of men and women were brought to Christ and lived to serve him. And in each case, marriage played a significant role in the development of that effectiveness.

My husband and I have had the chance to spend large amounts of time with young men and women called into ministry. We meet them in the flower of their enthusiasm for what lies ahead. The men seem often to be caught up with the great possibilities, the great convictions, and the great horizons. They anticipate conquering. But get some of the young wives aside for very long, and you might pick up an alternative perspective on expectations for the future.

I'm often disturbed by the dis-ease that lies deep in the heart of young wives. It isn't long before many of them confide their fear that they will not be adequate to keep pace with their husbands' dreams. They worry about getting along with people, about getting lost in the shuffle, about being unable to live up to all the ideals that Christianity calls people to fulfill. I'm also disturbed how apparently little thought is given in the world of pastoral training to help these wives overcome such fears.

If you sat with me in the middle of such a group of women and listened to the questions raised, you might be impressed that the same themes inevitably wend their way into most conversations. Whether it's New England or California, the subject matter rarely varies. Interestingly enough, they are the exact themes I have worked on myself during twenty years of ministry. And while they are not lengthy, they are highlights of pastoral marriage as Gordon and I have experienced them. And they are, again and again, the matters over which we have seen pastoral marriages fail.

The discussions almost always begin with the question of *priorities*. Uncommon unions are no accident. They are the result of two people having decided early in their marriage that their relationship as husband and wife will take precedence over all other relationships on a human level.

At least two things cemented that notion in our hearts. The first was the example my husband had observed in the home of a Presbyterian pastor and his wife, Dr. Frank and Helen Moss. During a highly impressionable period of his college life, Gordon had virtually lived in their home and watched with wonder the unwavering quality of their pastoral marriage.

How many times Gordon has recounted to me his memories of mealtimes at the Mosses and the quality of conversation that caused everyone at the table to grow. He was touched by the attempts both husband and wife made to put the other in a first-place position when it came to spending time working together, relaxing together, and serving others together.

A second impression that welded its way into our hearts was the simple, but stunning, observation made for us when we were just newlyweds trying to get our marital feet on the ground. We were attending a conference, and Gordon had a chance to spend a few moments with an older pastor who seemed to be a wellspring of wisdom. The question Gordon asked him seems almost shockingly naive to me today, but you have to remember that we grew up in a generation where one was often taught that everything was laid on the altar to serve God, even if that notion meant ignoring your spouse and your children to do whatever you perceived God's will to be.

So it was not altogether a stupid question at the time when Gordon asked, "Sir, what do you find to be the most important: your family or the Lord's work?" His answer set a pace for us that we have never broken. Looking rather sternly at Gordon, the older man answered, "My son, your family *is* the Lord's work."

Those and other early experiences taught us that the quality of our marriage must be a mutually shared effort. We would not *let* our marriage work; we would *make* it work. We believed that marriage, in order to reflect the love of Jesus Christ toward the Church, would demand an output of our peak energy. Also we realized that that priority relationship would probably always be a prime target for the enemies of Christ.

I am not reluctant to say that, next to my love for Jesus Christ, my marriage is my number one priority. My ministry is first and foremost directed toward my husband. I made a decision years ago to invest the largest percentage of my energies into his life. I have made myself a gift to him—that's a somewhat bold statement and may even be unpopular with some younger women today who have attached themselves to a new line of values that quest for "identity" and "independence." A little of both is, of course, important for all of us. But unlike some today, I determined early in our relationship that my identity would not be determined by my success in pursuing some outside vocation; rather, it would be found in developing relationships in which everybody involved grew according to his or her God-given potential.

Our marriage even comes before the church and its demanding schedule. Because of my husband's nature as a leader, it is very easy for him to get caught up in his work to the point that he loses perspective. He forgets how many hours he has put in on the job on a given day; he finds it hard to say no to people in, and outside, the church, when they ask for his attention and participation. He also finds it difficult at times to turn his mind off when it comes to solving problems, mentally writing sermons or manuscripts, or being concerned about the welfare of someone who is suffering from what seems to be an insoluble problem. I can be a balancing agent for him, calling him away from needless exhaustion and finding some creative way to get him to relax and absorb new strength. If I had other priorities in my life, I would quickly lose touch with his pace and rhythm, and I would be unable to sense when he needed to withdraw.

In my early adult years I had a vocation outside the home and maintained it until the end of our third year of marriage. Through that experience I came to know something of the world of the professional woman. I recognize that 55 percent of the female population today is involved in a career. Many of them would certainly be bored with staying at home and love doing what they do in an office or out in the marketplace.

If a career is our choice, then we must realize at least two things. First, the expectations of husband and wife for knowing each other's worlds in a marriage will probably be lowered. And second, the complementary "helpmate" aspect of marriage will have to be worked at even harder. If husband and wife pursue independent vocations, both will come home with the same needs. Often they will have to hurry to get the necessary work done at home so that they can simply hurry back to work outside the home. Something must be sacrificed, and it's often the depth of knowing each other fully in the marital relationship.

The pastor's wife who pursues an alternate vocation may defend it on the basis of financial need. That is doubtless a justification in many homes, and it may indeed be quite legitimate. But before we content ourselves with that reasoning alone, let's routinely assess whether we are working to take care of *needs* and not *desires*. Gordon and I deliberately chose to curtail our financial desires, channeling our energies into the ministry alone, and we believe we are the spiritually wealthier for it. We are sensitive to what D. R. Davis in *The Sin of Our Age* calls the "dogma of increasing wants."

This matter of vocation is among the priority choices each woman has to make. Having known a career earlier in my marriage, I still have chosen not to pursue it. That has been a happy choice for me and the perspective from which I now speak.

In a deeply moving article in *Leadership*, a journal for pastors, Dr. B. Clayton Bell relates the story of a tragedy he and his congregation faced when one of their families was virtually wiped out in the crash of a private plane. A father, two of his children, and a son-in-law were lost, leaving only the mother and one daughter. Bell recounts the process of pastoring he experienced when he went to the home and confronted a lovely Christian woman with the news that her family was gone.

Among the things that impressed me about his analysis of the experience was the participation of his wife, Peggy, who joined him in bringing comfort. She was able to spend long hours with the grieving widow. Clayton Bell wrote of her ministry:

> How grateful I am for a wife who is sensitive to others' hurts. Peggy's creative common sense and practical piety enabled her to do what was needed at the moment. Her gift had never been more apparent to me than in our *joint ministry* to Stephanie.[3]

And what was it that Peggy Bell was able to do? She describes a part of her role in ministering:

> Stephanie, wrapped in a robe, lay in her darkened room with her face buried in a pillow wet with tears. I sat on the edge of her bed and gently rubbed her shoulders or wiped her face with a cool damp cloth. She had asked not to be left alone; it was so important to be near and to hear anything she might want to say. . . .
>
> In the evenings Clayton and I frequently drove over to check on her. She talked, many times with tear-stained face, yet with great control, about her courtship, her wedding, vacation trips, problems, dreams, and plans. She talked about her children, the happy times and the sad times; she talked about their schooling, their training, their commitment to the Lord Jesus. Never once were we bored. . . .[4]

The significance of these lines is two-fold: A pastor and his wife worked together and the wife was able to add a perspective and a dimension to the pastor's ministry that he himself could never have accomplished. Looking back and using the experience as a teaching lesson, Bell wrote:

> I'm extremely grateful to the Lord for a wife who shares my ministry with me. Peggy's perceptions and sensitivity have been great assets in ministering. She is able to do for widows what would be inappropriate for me to do. *Because the Lord has equipped her with gifts, complementary to mine, I rejoice that we can share much of the ministry to bereaved people.* [5] (Italics mine)

That is only one example of the possibilities open to a pastor and his wife when they have a shared ministry. Each man and woman entering the pastoral lifestyle will have to wrestle with this matter. In the Clayton and Peggy Bell marriage, it's obvious that Peggy has made it her priority to become a complement to Clayton and his activities, while he has opened the door and acknowledged her desire and ability to help him.

I am probably more active in our congregation than the wives of a lot of pastors. That is partly because our children are now older and need less of my attention. It is also partly because our congregation has taken care of us at a financial level where there has been no need for me to worry about gaining extra income for the family. And of course I enjoy our people—I love them. But even my activity within the congregation is carefully limited because I saw long ago that my greatest ministry to our church would be in the provision of a home for their pastor. If I did my job at home, he would be able to come refreshed each day to serve the people who had called him to be their spiritual shepherd.

As part of my own principle of priority, I try to be fresh and at my best as a person when I know my husband is going to be available at home. That extends, as a rule, to the way I dress, to the way the house is kept, to the food I prepare, and to the mood in the home when he comes to it. Please don't think that I have perfected this pursuit of priority! Let me simply say that it is a goal to be pursued, one I keep foremost in my consciousness.

After a retreat at which I spoke, a lady in her forties came to me for advice. She seemed terribly frightened. Her daughter was about to get married, and her husband had purchased tickets for a Caribbean cruise so that the two of them could get away after the wedding for a "honeymoon" of their own. "Fantastic," I said, wondering what in the world the problem might be.

"No," she said, "there really is a problem. I don't know my husband anymore. We don't seem to have anything to talk about. Years ago he went his way and I went mine. My whole life has been wrapped up in my children. Now they're gone."

Her dilemma may seem to many to be unusual, but her theme is not. She's a victim of misplaced priorities, and so is her husband. For him the business came first; for her, just as tragically, the children came first. Now they are strangers. Their marriage has little to offer either one of them.

The principle of priority also comes into play when I consider my own personal schedule. As both a teacher and a speaker, I have carefully limited myself to a certain number of outside obligations each year. I once found it easy to fill an almost empty calendar a year in advance. Then when the scheduled times came, I would discover that there were all sorts of marital responsibilities which had to be left behind the last minute because I had not planned my time well. Thus I've learned the hard way that certain mealtimes, days, weekends, vacation times, and even special lunch times should be reserved so that my husband and I can share prime time together for the ongoing maintenance of our relationship.

Pursuing and developing a quality marital relationship is a type of gift to the people of the congregation whom we serve. I believe that congregations need models, symbols of hope and unity in the home that they can pursue for their own families.

The importance of this priority principle was impressed upon me several years ago when Gordon and I returned to my hometown of Aurora, Illinois. We were there to celebrate the fiftieth anniversary of the Wayside Cross Rescue Mission. The superintendent of the mission, Paul Johannaber, and his wife, Kay, had given twenty-five years of energy and service to the mission. The work of the Wayside Cross Mission had been so effective that the name and a picture of the mission were stamped upon the auto safety stickers which all Aurora cars had to display during that fiftieth anniversary year.

The *teamwork* of Paul and Kay Johannaber is one of the key factors in the great ministry of the Wayside Cross Mission. Years ago Kay Johannaber told me she realized that the heart of her husband was deeply committed to the work of the mission. Wishing to share that conviction with him, Kay returned to school and completed her nursing degree so that she could team up with her husband in a much more complete sense. Rather than to entertain feelings of neglect, she chose to participate in his vision and to marshal all of her strength behind his vision. In short, she shared it to the extent that it became her vision also. Today she heads the Women's Division of the Wayside Cross Mission and is quite effective in reaching needy women in the inner city of Aurora.

As I sit among young pastors' wives talking about the ministry, I am frequently impressed by how many questions center around the principle of *listening*.

In the twenty years that Gordon and I have shared the pastoral ministry, we've seen a frightening number of marriages fail and pastorates dissolve because a husband or a wife or both lacked the know-how or the desire to listen.

John Drakeford once wrote a book entitled *The Awesome*

Power of the Listening Ear. The title itself is a message to ponder. Immense power is derived from listening. Mary, the mother of our Lord, was able to serve as she did because she was more of a listener than a talker. She listened to the words of an angel who revealed God's plan to her. And rather than blurt it all out to anyone who was around,

> *Mary kept all these things, and pondered them in her heart.*
> (Luke 2:19, KJV)

Mary also listened when Jesus acknowledged his awareness of his Father's business. She listened as he taught and recruited his disciples. She showed that she understood the power of the listening ear when she told the servants at the wedding at Cana,

> *Do whatever he tells you.* (John 2:5)

I think that Gordon and I began our married life listening! Even before our wedding, we sought out wise and trustworthy people, sat them down, and asked them a variety of questions about: the great challenges they'd experienced in life; the accumulation of experience; ways of strengthening relationships; the conduct of ministry; and the maintenance of daily spiritual freshness. After listening, we had all the more to talk about when it came time for us to be alone together.

We quickly learned the importance of listening to each other—not only to the words, but also to one another's silences, moods, gestures, and actions. We began asking ourselves, "What does the other want me to hear?" During the early years of our marriage, Gordon was still a student in seminary. Occasionally after an unsettling lecture, he would come home, confused about some aspect of doctrine or theology. There were even times when he found himself struggling with doubt. Frankly, I think I handled him poorly at times. Rather than hearing him out and affirming him for sharing his inner thoughts, I was often shaken. I found myself—perhaps because of my own insecurities— blurting out, "How can you go into the ministry if you can't even take a stand on that issue?" Had I persisted with responses of that sort, I think I would have inadvertently taught Gordon to either keep his thoughts to himself or find someone else willing to understand. He needed neither my accusations nor even my attempted answers; he really only desired my listening ear.

On the other hand, Gordon had to learn to listen to me also. Because I really cared about how he came across to other people, I could often see ways in which he could have done things better or said things more gently to people. I tried to be his most loving critic when it came to being a sounding board for his sermons. I realized I could offer him thought-starters, illustrative materials, even, perhaps, an argument to challenge his logic or his conclusions.

Again, listening became a paramount principle. It was important not only that he be willing to listen to me, but also that I phrase my thoughts in such a way that he realized that I was sharing my ideas out of *love* and from a motive of enhancing his ministry rather than putting him down. The failure of many couples in the pastoral ministry to bring the best out in each other finds its cause right here. One does not know how to talk, and the other does not know how to listen.

There are certain times, I have learned, when Gordon finds it easier to listen to me than at other times. Sunday lunch is not a good time for me to critique a morning sermon. Usually Monday evening is better since the emotion of Sunday is drained off and he is less liable to be defensive. Moments when he is under extreme pressure due to staff difficulties or important decision making are not ordinarily listening moments for him. I've slowly learned over the years how to find just the right time, the right words, and the right approach. Just as slowly he, too, has learned the value of listening to what I've had to say. After years and years of working at it, we've forged a relationship that rarely gets short-circuited because of a deaf ear.

How many good men and women in leadership have failed because they refused to listen to their closest friends or even their enemies? Rather than listen for the kernel of truth that is in virtually every communication, too many have found it necessary to get the wagons of self-defense into a circle and fight back like the pioneers of old. Sooner or later such rigidity hurts a marriage. It inevitably hurts the ministry.

As I sit with groups of young pastors' wives, a third theme also regularly arises: the theme of *serving*. Perhaps it overarches all the others.

Servanthood as a biblical concept is uniquely Christian in that it is a quality of relationship that one *voluntarily* assumes. One of my major goals in life is to serve my husband. In short, I am committed to doing everything possible to see that every quality God has placed in his life is developed at least as far as I can personally make possible.

No service was below our Lord Jesus when he walked on the earth. He was servant to both the great and the lowly. He created a spiritual atmosphere in which many people grew. He expressed what he meant by washing the feet of his disciples.

No marriage needs the servanthood mind more than the pastoral marriage. This does not mean that one becomes a doormat for the other. Both must agree to the servanthood principle, and both are fulfilled as a result.

When I think of servanthood, I see it primarily as two people bringing out the best in each other. For me, serving my husband means freeing him up to pursue his gifts and his calling. If he can be liberated from nonessential details, from a score of little things that he isn't highly skilled at handling, he can then successfully master other things that he is good at.

A few years ago I suggested that Gordon take a couple of weeks of our vacation and write the draft of what became his first book. He had all the materials together; it was just a matter of getting the manuscript written. "I'll tell you what," I said, "you write from sun up to sun down. I'll keep things quiet, serve the meals, be around whenever you need me. But don't you think about one other thing until you get the book written." I kept my word. The chapters were written, and God has used that first book, *Magnificent Marriage*.

At Peace Ledge, we have many things growing in the forest near our home. It is amazing to me how things grow when the underbrush is cleared away and the quality trees and plants are permitted to expand. Measurable growth takes place within a matter of weeks. Servanthood is like that. Once we clear away the underbrush in life for each other, we can stand back and enjoy the growth.

It is quite clear to me now that Gordon was serving me a few years ago when he began to nudge me into a deeper search for my spiritual gifts. Knowing our children would need me less and less, he pushed me to read more, to study, and to think more deliberately about the themes of spiritual living that were important to me. And then one day when I was invited to speak at a women's retreat, he volunteered to stay with the children so that I could go. What had he been doing? Clearing away the "underbrush" of my life and releasing me to grow as God wanted me to in that dimension of my being.

Voluntarily laying aside my "rights" is an act of grace. No one does it naturally, and one is not often applauded for doing it. Nevertheless, it is the way of Christ!

When the principle of serving abounds in a marriage, a rigid sense of roles is not necessary. Perhaps whoever is best at mastering details and enjoys working with numbers might be the one to keep the finances. In our home, outside of cooking meals, I have really no sense of a "role" to fulfill. Work is work and whoever has the time and the opportunity to do it helps get it done. I have seen some homes where the husband is even the chef. Without a doubt, one of the most comforting pictures the Gospel writers give of our Lord is his first act after the resurrection when he cooked breakfast for his disciples.

Releasing one another to our highest God-given potential means that selfishness diminishes and giving increases. And we do so willingly, not grudgingly.

Years ago when cars were first manufactured, there was nothing called a "clutch." The grinding noise when gears were shifted was gruesome. Then someone invented a "sycromesh gear" which enabled the driver to shift easily and quietly. You could say that selfishness, a lack of serving, causes a grinding in the gears of marriage and that is certainly gruesome. There is a need for a sycromesh gear called *servanthood* in a relationship. And the more it is perfected, the smoother the "ride" and the less clashing there will be.

I recently read a biography of the great American leader and orator, Daniel Webster. By the age of thirty-one Webster had become known as one of America's most effective speakers. He was capable of presenting material in such a way that everyone could understand and be convinced of the truth that he was attempting to communicate. Webster had strong convictions against slavery, for example, and spoke out in favor of the abolition of slavery whenever possible.

One of Webster's earlier biographers, Norman Hapgood, assigns much of the great orator's success to the quality of his marriage to a woman, Grace Fletcher, whom he married at the age of twenty-six. Of her the writer says:

> She had the goal of keeping alert to those high principles which her husband held. Her upright New England faith and sweet loyalty must have been one of the strongest barriers resisting the temptations which lay before the impressionable statesman.[6]

When Grace Fletcher Webster died, Daniel remarried a year later. The biographer said of Carolyn Roy, his second wife:

> She brought him money and social position and nothing else that could be traced in his life.[7]

Two years into that second marriage it was said of Webster:

> He steadily declined from a height at which his altering nature could no longer sustain itself.[8]

Daniel Webster began overeating and drinking. His spending habits soared out of control, and his moral life disintegrated. By the end of his political life, the man once known for his great integrity had become typed as a political compromiser. Tragedy mounted upon tragedy, and when he died, he was a beaten and bitter man.

When did the change in Daniel Webster's life take place? One solid point at which the decline in Webster seems to have begun was at the death of his first wife, Grace, and his marriage to his second wife, Carolyn. As long as Grace had been alive, Daniel Webster had been an asset to the nation. It is frighteningly clear to me that his greatness was, to a large extent, fueled by that earlier servanthood-style of marriage. His second wife did nothing to build him up or to restrain him.

The fourth topic young pastors' wives often seem to be concerned about is *communication* in their homes. Typical questions sound like these: Is it possible, with the enormous demands placed upon anyone in leadership, for a husband and wife to adequately communicate? Will we have enough time to talk? Can I keep up with my spouse and how do I do it? Is there any way of knowing whether I will be a disappointment or an asset to him?

Communicating with a communicator can be frustrating at times. Like many others, I have a husband who often comes home at suppertime, having been involved in non-stop conversation with one person after another since early in the morning. The last thing in the world he really wants to do at that moment is to talk.

"What went on in your life today?" may get a response, but then again it may elicit little more than a grunt. I am reminded of the cartoon in which a pompous-looking businessman sits in an easy chair and glares over the top of his paper at a wife who has obviously just accused him of withdrawing from her. "I communicated at the office all day," he says. "Isn't that enough?"

Many years ago Walter Trobisch taught Gordon and me the importance of our communicating regularly through the use of what he called a "marital quiet time." He proposed that Gordon make it a habit to call from the office each day just before he left to come home. That would give me enough warning to expect him. That, Walter said, should be my cue to arrange affairs in the house so that when my husband arrived I could take ten or fifteen minutes, drop everything and visit with him.

Ever since Trobisch suggested the use of a marital quiet time, we've deliberately pursued that as an objective. Usually I meet Gordon at the door with cool juice, and we retreat to the living room for a brief time in which to share our day. Trobisch had said, "Your wife has worked in your home all day long, Gordon, to purchase your right to work outside of it. . . . Now it is your responsibility to share with her what her work has set you free to accomplish."

We've learned much from that advice and have pursued that principle of communication for several years. Granted, when children are young, it's hard to plan unbroken minutes like the kind we now enjoy. In those days we were careful to plan longer, though less frequent, quiet times when we got away from everything for a day at a time. We sometimes called it "buying a memory." In order to do that, we had to plan extensive quiet times way ahead on our calendars.

Even now in our home we will take our calendars every six weeks and deliberately mark off days and evenings for the next two months when family and marriage times will be a top priority. When others later ask us to do something at those designated times, we simply respond, "Sorry, we already have a commitment." Because Gordon and I respect those commitments to one another, I'm not disturbed when he has to give added time to the church in an emergency. I know where his heart really lies. But in a general sense communication happens in our home because we take the time to communicate.

Then again, communication has been enhanced in our home because we hold suppertime to be virtually inviolable. Our children know, as does Gordon, that suppertime is family time. There we can look forward to being with each other, draw each other out, and hear about one another's life with God and with the rest of the world. Generally we permit no intrusions into this time, except for an occasional guest our children bring (and they are always welcomed) or an out-of-town visitor who may be ministered to by our hospitality. The telephone is always removed from the hook for that hour.

When my husband has a late board meeting or I anticipate that he will have a difficult evening ahead of him, I try to order my day so that I get enough afternoon rest to stay up late and welcome him home. He is generally wide awake and reflective, and I am eager to share the ideas, dreams, and disappointments that he may bring home with him at a late hour.

Sheldon Vanauken in his book, *A Severe Mercy*, impressed me with his insight that the most memorable times we share in a marriage are those moments when time is of little concern. Could it be, he muses, that in moments when time is forgotten, we are experiencing a small measure of eternity's timelessness? In such a context our spirits are free to commune with one another and we learn so much more.

A pastor always has to be searching for the hidden agenda in the lives of those to whom he ministers. Why not the same in a marriage? Indeed we have tried, and we are quick to do things such as making frequent phone calls to one another and writing cards expressing love and encouragement when one of us is facing a day full of stress.

When I have gone off on our annual women's retreat, Gordon has traditionally placed love notes in my bedroll, my luggage, and my Bible. Occasionally they have been poetic in form, and the women of our congregation have become curious about their contents. Each year it has become increasingly intriguing and even hilarious to find out what the pastor and his wife have going between them now in their communication.

Take, for example, this piece of silly communication between the two of us:

The Ode of a Lonesome Husband

Whenever I consider
how this lonely night is spent,
I find myself perplexed
on why my wife has "went."

There she is in Sunapee
and we must be apart
just forty miles separate
but love makes that a lot.

Here, tonight alone, my dear,
the bed is very cold.
There, you'll curl up in your bag.
We two have none to hold.

I wish it were all a football game

and now there'd be a huddle;
so while the quarterback called the play
we'd have the time to cuddle.

I love you.

Gordon's poetry usually has a lot more quality than that sample of intimate communication, but it is crazy, hastily scribbled lines like those which enhance the freshness of a special marital love affair that never lacks for joy.

The Lord has given my husband a chance to travel more and more frequently, and we've tried to work hard at keeping our communication effective even while apart. It is not unusual for each of us to hand the other a stack of cards, separately dated for each of the days we are apart. A card usually includes a verse of Scripture or a quote from some piece of religious literature or simply an affirmation or prayer concerning the anticipated events of the days during which we will be separated.

Recently Gordon left hurriedly on an around-the-world trip; the first stop was London. While there, he was the dinner guest of his friend, Tom Phillips, the chairman of Raytheon Corporation. Unable to write all the notes he wanted to give me before he left and knowing that Mr. Phillips would be returning to our hometown of Lexington the next day, Gordon asked him if he would mind having a package of notes delivered to me when he got back at the Raytheon offices. You can imagine my amazement when two days later a uniformed chauffeur arrived at the church office and delivered a package of love notes. I wonder whether he was aware that all he was bringing to an ordinary person like me was a package of notes that a preacher traveling in Europe wanted to get to his wife for the sake of good communication!

When I join young women who are the wives of pastors, there are the inevitable questions concerning the nature of conflict in a pastoral marriage. A few seem surprised when I comment that conflict will always exist even in the happiest and most effective marriages. But as my husband wrote in his book, *Magnificent Marriage,* the key is whether the conflict is destructive or constructive. The decision belongs to the marital partners.

We have found that it is very easy for conflict to get out of control in a pastor's home. Since ministry is spiritual warfare, the Enemy of Christ would love nothing better than to tempt pastors and Christian leaders to leave their marital relationships in disarray each day as they go out to serve the Body of Christ. How can men and women in leadership preach sermons, witness to their faith, and counsel broken people if there is dissension or an unresolved conflict back in their homes?

It's for that reason that Gordon and I quickly learned to keep short accounts in our marriage. We resolved not to allow silence to become a part of our conflicts. We chose never to leave one another angry. And we pledged that forgiveness would become a significant way of life. The Apostle Paul understood the importance of forgiveness when he wrote:

> *Do not let the sun go down on your anger.* (Ephesians 4:26)

C. S. Lewis also understood it when he wrote, "Love leaves a clean wound." He seemed to be sensitive to the fact that a relationship becomes quickly infected if it is not cleansed through the conflict-resolving act of forgiveness.

I have never forgotten a wise professor of psychology at the University of Denver and his analogy between relationships and silverware. The two—silverware and relationships—are purchased at great cost and are therefore precious, he said. They are both useful and are also capable of becoming easily tarnished. Unless regularly polished, silverware quickly grows dull and unsightly. It needs a soft cloth, gentle stroking, and the cleansing effect of tarnish remover. Then he added that forgiveness and confession are the tarnish removers in all relationships.

You don't clean silver objects with Brillo pads, and you do not cleanse relationships with the abrasiveness of anger, resentment, or vindictive words. How sad to see a piece of silver neglected for years. It is so blackened that one is hard put to believe that the silver item was ever attractive or desirable. How often a husband looks at a wife or she at him and says quietly, "What did I ever find attractive in that person?" The silver may still be there, but what has changed is the quality of the care. If the beauty of tarnished relationships is to be recovered, it will be done only by the gentle stroking of forgiveness and confession.

Most of the conflicts between Gordon and me have been resolved because both of us wanted our relationship to grow. It has been important to remind ourselves in the midst of conflict that neither one of us really wants to hurt or damage the other deliberately. And if the moment has been too painful, either one of us has sometimes resorted to sitting down and writing out feelings and attitudes on paper. In this way we've learned to keep our conflicts to a minimum and to resolve those which threaten to get out of control.

The importance of the principle of short accounts and polished silver is not to be underestimated, I like to remind my young friends. An ugly, but necessary, fact to face is that a congregation can often possess one or two who are only too glad to take advantage of a bad relationship in the pastor's home and provide the temptations that can destroy a pastor's marriage and his ministry.

Many conversations about pastoral marriages often center on the question of how a wife can keep herself intellectually and spiritually on the growing edge. Many of us realize all too well that it is very easy for a woman to turn off a large part of her mind during the years of young motherhood.

The cries of her baby, the smell of soiled diapers, and the need for food preparation tend to drown out the groans of an unread book. It becomes increasingly easy for a wife to forget newspapers, the arts, literature, and the world of ideas in which her husband is involved—even the study of the Word of God itself. I have been able to maintain this part of my life partially because I have a sweeping curiosity and partially because my husband has freed me to develop my mind.

As I mentioned earlier, I cannot overemphasize the importance of a woman stimulating and sharpening her own inner spirit. While I might have been tempted to do so in earlier years, I cannot live on my husband's spirituality. All too often he has asked me to lead the family in our devotional exercises. I *have* to be ready. And more than once I have been able to find from reading Scripture and the great Christian mystics, insights that have also been helpful to him.

Both my prayer life and the keeping of a journal have kept me inwardly alive. Beyond those, I have pressed myself hard to keep reading. If I hear my husband or somebody else repeatedly referring to a particular book, I try to obtain a copy of it. And I have rarely been disappointed when I read it through. Occasionally I have taken an entire day to do nothing but read and study. Please don't misunderstand me—such a thing was a virtual impossibility when our children were small. But things are different now, and I have been able to build a filing system made up of loose-leaf topical notebooks in which I keep my thoughts and insights. All of this has become a kind of mental and spiritual garden in which I can grow ideas for later development and use.

As I've said before, one's mind is to be kept alive through asking questions and listening for answers. Too many men are ignorant of the fact that women also want to learn. Gordon and I have been sadly impressed a number of times when fine men of God have entered our home for a meal or conversation and have tended to ignore me. Rarely have they ever looked in my direction, choosing rather to direct all their conversation to my husband, apparently assuming that I was not interested in what they had to say.

I have the kind of husband who notices things like that. More than once I have seen him get up at the end of a meal and insist that the guest and I stay seated, while he proceeded to clear the table and load the dishwasher. What was happening? My husband was forcing our guest to talk with me alone. Invariably the quality of the conversation has changed noticeably through the remainder of the evening because the guest quickly learned that I too was interested in who he was and in what he had to say and would like to be a part of the fellowship he had to offer.

I have a wonderful mother whose quiet, generous spirit has taught me much about the art of giving. As an outgrowth of that learning, I love to give my friends gifts on birthdays and anniversaries. It occurred to me one day that one of my opportunities as the wife of a pastor was to give gifts to my husband. And so now I often challenge young wives to ask themselves, "What gifts can I give my husband that he probably will not be able to receive from any other source?"

Let me list a few that occur to me. One of the greatest gifts I think I can give Gordon is my trained *sensitivity* or *intuition*. I am not prepared to argue whether or not that is innate or culturally created, but I'll use it whenever possible. As a woman, I am a "feeler"; I can sense things and situations that Gordon may be tempted to overlook. I sense the meaning of eye contact, rigidity, and the meaning of distance when I'm with people. Over the years Gordon has apparently learned to sound out my impressions of people when I'm with him. He and I both know that I'm not infallible, but I do offer a second opinion which he evidently values.

I also bring my husband the gift of *protection*. I think I've learned when it is wise to screen his calls and urge the caller to call back or arrange for a later return of the message. If we have had long stretches of company, I can sense Gordon beginning to withdraw inwardly. His inner spirit quickly needs rest and filling. I am usually the one who will urge him "to go north," as we say it in our family, and spend a day or two at our New Hampshire retreat where he can get back into the Scriptures and spend time in meditation.

Charles Haddon Spurgeon recognized this need:

> Rest time is not waste. It is economy to gather fresh strength. Look at the mower in the summer's day, with so much to cut down ere the sun sets. He pauses in his labor—is he a sluggard? He looks for his stone, and begins to draw it up and down his scythe, with renk-a-tink, renk-a-tink. Is that idle music—is he wasting precious moments? How much might he have mowed while he had been ringing out those notes of his scythe! But he is sharpening his tool, and he will do far more when once again he gives his strength to those sweeps which lay the grass prostrate in rows before him. Nor can the fisherman be always fishing; he must mend his nets. So even our vacation can be one of the duties laid upon us by the kingdom of God.[9]

A wife who does not protect her husband may watch him burn out emotionally or spiritually long before his time. And that is why I prayerfully and carefully watch for misdirected priorities, long periods of unnatural silence, overinvolvement in tasks and underinvolvement in relationships. I watch for a dwindling of the caring instinct, a draining of the joy for his work, the tendency to react rather than to initiate, an increasing lack of judgment or wisdom and, of course, an empty spirit. It goes without saying that my husband is equally concerned about those possibilities in me.

One other aspect of protection is that of my being his source of physical affection and pleasure. He and I have grieved over the many pastoral marriages which broke up because of sexual infidelity. Frankly, both of us believe that in most cases the sexual unfaithfulness was a result, and not a cause, of the marital failure.

Unfaithfulness is sin and cannot be glossed over or excused before God. But all too often it happens because a husband and a wife have not brought gifts to one another. The husband has not found a haven of rest in his wife's arms. Freedom of expression, joy, passion, appreciation, and celebration of relationship have been missing. In their place have been the drabness of unacceptance, coldness, and thanklessness. In such cases it is only a matter of time before one partner or the other yields to the great temptation to draw companionship from another source.

Many Christian leaders have pointed out that there is a close parallel between the spiritual and sexual drives within us. The result is that when one works closely with people in a caring, emotional context, the risks of physical contact are more likely to be increased. Rather than resent a husband's counseling or grow jealous of it, a pastor's wife can be careful to understand it. She need not feel competitive with others; she can be careful to maintain the kind of relationship with her husband which is always fresh and renewing. She should try very hard to build a trusting, nonmanipulative relationship that says, "He picked me. I'll make him glad he did!"

Sometimes at the end of a long evening of typical conversation with young pastors' wives, I'll find myself making one final point which I press with urgency. "Let the man you love and believe in dream his dreams," I say. "Dream with him, and cushion him whenever there is a disappointment or a failure."

There is a delicate balance that a godly wife must maintain, and I can only suggest that it depends upon the gift of wisdom. That wisdom consists in knowing when to encourage a man to take risks and surge ahead in spite of the odds and when to help him face the reality that perhaps his dreams are born of wrong motives, wrong objectives, and wrong capabilities. A wife cannot be expected to be right on every occasion, but she can be a trusted source when evaluation is necessary. For that, she needs to be a woman of prayer, a person endowed with the discernment of God's Holy Spirit.

As you know, I love to see things grow. In my spare moments I am often outside pulling weeds, fertilizing, and watering so that things like flowers and tomato plants can grow to the fullness of their beauty and taste. In a deeper way I love to see the growth of human beings—my children, other believers, the people who enter our home and receive our hospitality. Primarily, though, I love to see my husband grow, and if I have anything to do with it, he'll continue to grow until the day God takes him home. And as God chooses, that growth will be in part because I have come alongside and helped to prepare the environment in which he matures to be more and more like Christ.

Few women in our generation of Christian living are worthy of more admiration than Ruth Bell Graham, the wife of Billy Graham. I have never met Mrs. Graham, but I have read her poetry frequently and carefully. We even named our New Hampshire retreat "Peace Ledge" after some lines in one of her poems.

Much of Mrs. Graham's poetry combines the kind of joy and honest melancholy that perhaps only the wife of a man in ministry can fully understand. Hers could be called a bittersweet experience: sweet because she has seen her husband represent Jesus Christ across the entire world; bitter, perhaps, because the cost to her and her homelife has been great. Still she doesn't complain. The product has been well worth the price, and her momentary sadness has brought others much joy and relief.

I have often wondered what events loom behind the words of her poem:

Love without clinging;
Cry—
If you must—
But privately cry;
The heart will adjust
To the newness of loving
In practical ways;
Cleaning and cooking
And sorting out clothes,
All say, "I love you,"
When lovingly done.

So—
Love without clinging;
Cry—
If you must—
But privately cry;
The heart will adjust
To the length of his stride,
The song he is singing,
The trail he must ride,
The tensions that make him
That man that he is,
The world he must face,
The life that is his.

So love
Without clinging;
Cry—
If you must—
But privately cry;
The heart will adjust
To being the heart,
Not the forefront of life;
A part of himself,
Not the object—
His wife.

So—
Love! [10]

I hear what she's saying, and I agree. She is speaking of an uncommon union. It is worth working for. It is delightful to possess. I know. I have one.

8
PK's Can Be OK

If I could get to the highest place in Athens, I would lift up my voice and say, "What mean ye, fellow citizens, that ye turn every stone to scrape wealth together and take so little care of your children to whom ye must one day relinquish all?"
Socrates, 450 B.C.

A FEW years ago my husband was asked to consider an invitation to leave the pastoral ministry and assume the leadership of an organization for which we have much affection and respect. It was a difficult decision. Both of us prayed about it, discussed it, and agonized over it in our private thoughts. There were times when making the move seemed to be the right thing, but there were also many moments when we felt exactly the opposite.

There came a moment in our decision making when we wondered whether our children could shed some light on the matter. We hadn't burdened them with the dilemma which had captivated our minds. What would they say if they knew about the possibility of our moving to another part of the country? Thus at Thursday evening's supper Gordon shared what was on our minds with Mark and Kristi. He somewhat sweetened the deal and defied the principle of objectivity by suggesting a number of things that might be possible because of the move. A horse for Kristi, perhaps? Proximity to a part of the country that had always intrigued Mark. What did they think?

There was silence in our kitchen. I could sense the wheels turning in two young minds. Then Mark said, "You mean that Dad wouldn't be a pastor anymore?"

"That's right, son," my husband replied. "The family would probably get to go to a church where you'd hear someone else preach. Think of it this way, you wouldn't always be known as a PK."

Surely, I could sense my husband thinking, that would attract any boy or girl who'd always lived in the congregational spotlight. But it didn't. Neither I nor Gordon was quite prepared for the way our children responded.

"I'm not sure I want to go to a church where Dad's not a pastor," one said.

"How could you leave here? Look how much these people love us and how much they've done for us!"

"No way. Dad's a pastor, and we're a pastor's family. Let's not go any other place."

I guess we should have known better than to consult such biased children. We'd taught them to love the servant life of the pastorate, and now they were handing the teaching back! In retrospect I realize that we shouldn't have been surprised by their reaction. Both children had shown tremendous loyalty to the two congregations they'd known in their lifetimes. Leaving our Midwestern congregation to come to New England had been an enormous shock for Mark and Kristi. It had taken a long time for them to face the fact that the people we left could get along without us.

A year after we left the people in Illinois, eight-year-old Kristi returned for a brief visit. When she came back home, I could sense that something was weighing heavily upon her mind. When her father got home that evening, she took him into the living room and sat down beside him.

"Daddy," she started, "the people in Illinois really miss

you. They're disappointed that you're not there. The people here are getting along fine. But out there they need you to come back. Daddy, would you please go back at least for a little while?"

It was hard for us to convince an eight-year-old that pastors were dispensable and that a congregation could make it without a former pastor returning to take over again.

Our children have known two happy congregations. To this day, they assume that most churches are pleasant places where people are usually supportive and united. And, frankly, if they feel that way, it's because we've worked hard to let them see that a congregation is God's advanced view of the heavenly lifestyle. It is a place where Christ's lordship should be in full view. And in such circumstances people—children included—should be able to find vast opportunities to grow to be whatever God has designed them to be.

When I begin to brood over what it takes to create an atmosphere in which the children of a pastor's family can find joy, I discover that many of the same categories which I covered in the previous chapter about marriage are helpful in thinking through other issues. My thinking about children in a pastor's home always starts with the same *principle of priorities*. "Your family *is* the Lord's work," the old preacher had told my husband. It's a joint ministry which Gordon and I share, and after the priority of our own marital relationship has been settled, our relationship to our children ascends in importance before anything else.

At the top of the list of priorities has always been our *determination to use discretionary time properly*. As I've noted already, we maintain a family calendar. Among the first items recorded when we project the use of our time in the coming months are the events that are important to our children's lives. We make time to be with them individually and jointly; to be part of their school events; and to support them in their special projects.

Many pastors and wives find it easy to complain about the busyness of their schedules. But few have ever considered the fact that their busy schedules are also flexible. If he so chooses, a pastor can take time off in an afternoon to be with a son or a daughter if he has planned carefully.

Gordon and I have made it a point to be on the sidelines of virtually every game in which either one of our children has been involved. Gordon has chosen to be a spectator, never a coach or any other form of leader, at all athletic events. This is the children's world, he reasons. There has to be some place where they see their father as a spectator and not as the one in charge.

Both he and I share vivid memories of a Friday afternoon when Kristi was playing during her first year of organized soccer. Her coach, a somewhat young and immature high school athlete, had shifted her from her normal position as a halfback to the fullback defensive position. A ball bounced down the field through several stumbling players. Kristi moved to her right to kick it. Just as she pulled back her leg, the goalie yelled at her to let it go, but she could not quite check her kick. The result was a tapping of the ball with her toe that changed the ball's direction and sent it past the goalie's hands and into the goal, giving a score for the other team.

Gordon and I watched as the insensitive girls on the team rushed back to where Kristi was standing and yelled, "You jerk, you've lost the game for us." The coach, using the break in the game to change players, unwisely substituted someone else for Kristi, compounding her feeling that she had failed and increasing her sense of embarrassment. We watched her run toward the sidelines. Then suddenly her eye caught Gordon's, and she veered in his direction. Burying her face in his stomach, she sobbed uncontrollably, "I didn't mean to do it."

Gordon and I looked at each other as if to ask, "What might have happened had we not been here?" But we had been there! Of the twenty-two players on the field, only four, including Kristi, had parental spectators on the side-lines to witness the good and the bad moments of the game, to share the ups and downs of their worlds. In part, our being there was the result of the flexibility of our schedule and the priority we had placed on our youngsters.

There is *priority in the area of attitudes* also. If our children have not been turned off by the pastoral lifestyle, perhaps it is because we have tried to reflect a positive perspective on all things. We've wanted them to learn that if anything is worth doing, it is worth doing with a positive view and to God's glory.

It may seem that I'm stretching a point, but I thought it important to set their priority in motion when our children were still in their cribs. As infants awakening from their sleep, they were greeted with a song and a smile. Mealtimes were deliberately punctuated with joy and a spirit of thank-fulness. Harsh words or critical attitudes were simply not welcomed at our table, and we made that very plain. When our children were old enough to become responsible for their actions and words, we would habitually ask a grouchy or critical Mark or Kristi to leave the room and come back to do an instant replay. For example, if one child entered the kitchen and complained, "Are we having that again for supper?" he or she might be requested to leave the kitchen.

"Now what I want you to do is come back in and say (with ultradramatic gestures and exaggerated enthusiasm), 'Oh, boy! We get to have that again for supper!' " Negative attitudes and critical spirits usually have been dissolved in laughter through such instant replays. And in game-playing of that sort, our children have always learned a better way.

But even a simple principle like that goes back to the thoughts of an earlier chapter. *These things happen only when people carry a spirit of thankfulness and honor at every moment.* Children learn not to turn up their noses at food or bargain basement clothing when they have learned that everything should first be handled with a sense of gratitude.

Since positive attitudes of thankfulness and joy engender

generosity, we've tried to teach our children the importance of giving. Every garage sale (and New England is famous for them) is a chance to show our children what happens when people turn from the generous attitude of giving things away to the needy and feel compelled to sell what often is really junk, hoping to retrieve one more dollar.

A child is given a wristwatch as a gift. The question then emerges: To whom shall he give the old watch? Why shouldn't he be encouraged to pray and to ask the Lord to bring the name of a person to mind who would benefit from such a gift?

People in our congregations have been very good to our children. One family gave our son a used trumpet when he began learning how to play one. Another man gave him some used darkroom equipment when he took an interest in photography. One special set of "grandparents" has been sending both children complete sets of the annual issues of American stamps for their birthdays. Those occasions and others have been times for our children to learn the joys of thankfulness and generosity. In part, the pastoral style of life has made it possible.

Occasionally I've felt that all of us were flagging in our attitude of thankfulness at home. Concerned that we face that problem squarely, I set up a "thankfulness jar." Each time someone did something for another, we would note it on a piece of paper and drop it into the jar. At the end of the week we would open the jar and read what had been deposited. We'd have a special time of rejoicing as the hidden and quiet things that we'd been doing for each other were noticed and given high profile.

A few weeks ago I was once again reminded about the importance of the spirit of thankfulness which my parents gave me. My father and mother had journeyed all the way from their Texas home to spend time with us in New England. During the time of their visit my Dad began to make us a grandfather's clock to add to the many handmade gifts of love that he and my mother have given us through the years of our marriage. While cutting a piece of wood with an electric saw, he accidentally cut off the ends of two fingers.

On the way to the hospital, he said to my mother, "Well, honey, look at it this way. I won't have to clean those fingernails anymore." Certainly there is the hint of a thankful spirit bursting through such pained humor.

Another priority attitude we've pursued in our pastoral home is that of *consistency*. The home of a minister is one in which children have a good chance to see both parents at work. Chances are that they will quickly pick up any hint that a mother or father is waivering in a commitment to Christ or to his work.

Even vacations subtly tell our offspring how serious our commitment is. A curious remark was made about our Lord:

> *And he came to Nazareth, where he had been brought up; and he went to the synagogue,* as his custom was. . . . (Luke 4:16)

Our children will "catch" whether our habits are born of conviction or are job-oriented. Do we visit a congregation for worship on the Lord's Day when we're on vacation? My husband has taught his own congregation that a regular routine of worship is very important in the Christian experience. The regularity of our own family worship during those periods of the year when our congregation does not see us or when we are not being paid to be on site teaches our children an important lesson about the consistency of our own convictions.

When I think of the consistency principle, I'm also concerned about it in terms of the atmosphere of our home. Because of our hectic schedule we've had to work hard to keep our children's schedule as consistent as possible. One of God's great gifts to us was a young woman, Lynn Schmacker, who for many years virtually lived in our home and became a big sister to our children whenever she was needed. Lynn refused money, believing that her work was her ministry for the Lord. She requested a monthly plan of our needs and would always arrive at the right time to care for our children. Lynn maintained an air of stability in which they could feel secure.

When Gordon and I had to be gone for an evening, Lynn considered it her responsibility to make sure that the children had consistent meals, bedtimes, discipline, and spiritual training. So impressive was her discipling in their lives that now, eight to ten years later, we still see very definite and measurable signs of her personality in our children's way of doing things.

Interestingly enough, God has rewarded Lynn Schmacker in response to her voluntary ministry in our lives. She has gone on to become a state-certified foster mother for five emotionally handicapped children. We have watched her care for children who had been tragically abused (and thus had been removed from their parents) and restore them to emotional and physical health.

"What is the key to the normalization of an abused child?" I once asked Lynn. She gave me one simple answer: consistency.

"Children find security in a predictable atmosphere," Lynn affirmed. She first tested that principle in our home and showed that it worked.

A pastor's home needs consistency in terms of discipline also. One of our close friends, David Howard, a missionary leader and author, comes from the unusual Howard family where all five sons and daughters have chosen to lead lives of highly effective service to the glory of God. One day when David was visiting Gordon and me, I asked him what he thought was the outstanding characteristic of his parent's conduct in raising such a great family. He quickly recalled his father's motto when it came to raising children: "Delayed obedience is disobedience."

Apparently Phillip Howard, David's father, did not believe in counting to five or ten when he asked his children to respond to his requests. He expected an immediate response to his word and he was consistent in that expectation. David Howard noted that it had been the consistency of his father's expectations which had made it easier for him as an adult to obey the heavenly Father.

In the semipublic home of a pastor, children need to learn who is in charge and whose word is final. That knowledge also brings security, which in turn makes it easier for each one to grow.

When the atmosphere of authority is uncertain and unclear, people grow uneasy. I saw this vividly illustrated just a few months ago when I went to watch Mark, our seventeen-year-old, play in a town league soccer game. The referee had not appeared at the game through a mixup in communications, and the coaches (young college boys) agreed that they would officiate until the referee arrived. The game was a disaster. I later wrote in my journal:

> What a lesson in leadership! Whistles were blown half-heartedly; the substitute "refs" could be talked out of a call; the boys played terribly; arguments broke out; one boy quit and walked off. A disaster! Having no one in charge meant that no one had a good time because anarchy broke out. Whether a game without a ref, a child without limits, or a church without a leader, the result is the same. Like this game, it is a sick reproduction of the real thing.

Because I'd been at the game, Mark and I had a good opportunity to discuss the "event." Subsequently whenever he's been tempted to resent authority in our family, I've been able to remind him of that game during which authority had been nonexistent. It has consistently helped him get the point!

In the list of priorities we've tried to maintain in our home, there is the strong sense of *ministry toward our children*.

How easy it is to forget, as we minister to the congregation, that our children also need to be pastored, to be given special spiritual attention. When our Lord was trying to show his disciples the importance of children, he said:

> *Whoever receives one such child in my name receives me; but whoever causes one of these little ones who believe in me to sin, it would be better for him to have a great millstone fastened round his neck and to be drowned in the depth of the sea.* (Matthew 18:5, 6)

Those are strong words! But within them lies the secret to loving even during those times when mothering in a pastor's home might seem mundane or repetitive.

A mother of six children once said to me, "It takes maturity to deal with the 'obscurity' of motherhood." She's right. And it also takes maturity to realize that *Christ himself is in our children*. It is Christ I am serving when I give my strength and affection to my son and my daughter.

A chance to visit the island of Jamaica several years ago brought me to the home of the Reverend and Mrs. Elmer Thompson. God had used them to found the effective West Indies Mission (now called Worldteam), which began out of their missionary home in Cuba fifty years ago. The Thompsons are not only the pioneers of a great missionary enterprise, but also the parents of five beautiful sons and daughters who have grown up to serve the Lord. Living in the Thompson home for several days, I caught the spirit of their devotion and prayer. That was obviously the kind of atmosphere appropriate for raising godly children. Mrs. Thompson told me that she believed her gift to the world was to raise children in whose hearts Christ was Lord.

I think my husband was a bit surprised when I phoned him from Miami on my way back home and said, "Honey, I'd like to consider having more children—to give more 'gifts' to the world." It was a noble notion, but after I got my feet on the ground, I realized that it wasn't the best course for us.

Nevertheless, seeing Christ potentially in my children has given me real joy in wanting to serve them in a way which would prepare and release them to be all that God intends them to be as gifts to the world. I hope my attitude has conveyed to them that even though I want to serve everyone God brings across my path, *they* are among the very first to get the best that I have to offer.

Seeing Christ in the children God gives us enables us to accept the process of life and not expect perfection. E. Stanley Jones once said that perfectionists are anxious and tense, demanding the impossible and getting the possible with disappointment. However, the Lord is different:

> *He does not raise his voice! He does not crush the weak, or quench the smallest hope. . . .* (Matthew 12:19, 20, TLB)

I can still clearly remember how hard those so-called "irrational" years were when the children were small. Sometimes I'd become weary of disciplining and discipling them. One day I wrote in my journal:

> I feel as if so much of my time is spent in doing nothing but saying no to the children. I wish I could see myself as Mrs. Brady on the "Brady Bunch" television program. But all too often I find myself looking like an ogre or some sort of Simon Legree. That discourages me. When will the day of response take place? And when will I be able to reason with the children instead of always seeming to say no to them?

All of us lose our capacity to see the finished product from time to time when we're working with people. But seeing Christ in our children gives us new hope for them and ourselves. A Southern pastor once said, "Hold a crown a few inches above your children's heads and then watch them grow into it."

When you and I begin to view them with Christ's eyes, we are able to see their Christ-given potential and then the direction of the process of growth. In fact, we produce what we believe in. Our Lord's patience with his disciples has often given me a renewed ability to hang on regardless of how frustrated I may feel. In the early years of motherhood my test centered on my ability to hold on to the growth process. Now, ironically, in the later years of motherhood, my test seems to be in letting go so that my children may complete their growth!

If *listening* is a key to a substantial marital relationship, it *is just as important when it comes to raising children in a pastor's home*. It's obvious that my husband and I are listening to everybody else. Do we listen to our children? They see their father stand in the front of a church sanctuary, shake hands, smile, and listen to anyone who seeks him out. Do they feel as if they get the same treatment? In a home which is often in "public view," it is extremely important to be sensitized to those moments which my husband calls the time of the "open window," when a child snaps up the shade that is over his or her heart and lets you take a peek inside.

"Open-window moments" can come at rather predictable times—during sickness or mounting pressures at school or a time of failure with friends or at mealtimes or bedtimes. If we, as parents, have an open ear, we may hear some wonderful insights or searching questions from our children. Unfortunately, the working mother or the too busy husband isn't always around to take full advantage of those thoughts.

When Kristi was seven, she had long blond hair that easily got tangled because of the overly active play life she pursued. One night when she was trying to get to sleep, I sat on the edge of the bed and rubbed her back, a tradition started when she was younger. She observed, "You know, Mom, tangles in your hair are like sin."

"Oh," I responded. "In what way?"

"Well, both hurt when you try to get rid of them," she said. "But if you don't get rid of them quickly, they can really mess things up, and they get harder and harder to comb out."

It was a sermon I'd never have to preach to her. She'd said it all herself, and by sharing it with me, we both knew that she had a sense of the importance of "short accounts" when it came to dealing with sin in her life. No baby-sitter would have stayed around long enough to appreciate that open-window moment. Perhaps the world will suggest that there are better things for a woman to be doing with her time, but I can hardly think of anything more significant. My listening to and affirming insights which I heard that night at Kristi's bedside may have sealed in her heart a life-long awareness of a very important spiritual principle.

Kristi is a teenager now, and a few months ago she had to make an important decision. It was an open-window moment. We wanted her to know that we trusted her judgment, but we also wanted to be available as a sounding board if she needed us. I watched my husband handle the situation and I learned from it. There had come a point in the process of decision making when he realized that she did not have the accumulated years of wisdom to make up her own mind. She was feeling peer pressure, and the battle was on between her convictions and their opinions.

The two of them sat talking in the living room. Then Gordon asked her, "Honey, do you think of yourself as an oak tree or a tulip?"

"What do you mean?" she asked.

"Well, an oak tree can be fully grown and strong. It's so big that people walk around it. No one steps on it. But a tulip can also be grown up; nevertheless, it's quite vulnerable. A tulip is beautiful to look at, of course, but it can be stepped on. Which do you think you are in this decision?"

"I'm a tulip, Daddy, and you know it," she said with tears.

It was an important moment for Kristi and her father. He and I had always assumed that she saw herself as strong and impervious to any outside pressure. Now she was admitting that she wasn't—at least at that moment.

"Sometimes tulips need a fence to be built around them to protect them so that they can continue to grow," Gordon suggested. "Perhaps this is one of those times when God has given you a father to perform like a fence, and the best way I can perform, in fact, is to tell you what I think the wisest decision would be, although in the final analysis you'll have to make it for yourself."

Kristi saw the wisdom of her father's proposal and subsequently embraced it. Once again both he and I saw the importance of our being in a place where we could listen and ask questions that would draw out cries for help. It may be that Kristi will look back for the rest of her life on that one important window moment, having derived from it a principle or two that will help her to make dozens of decisions throughout her adulthood.

Because of the busyness of a pastoral lifestyle in which telephones intrude and people yell loud for attention, it is emphatically important that a husband and a wife committed to ministry also take prime time to listen to what their children are saying and, of course, to *what they're not saying*.

In a pastoral home it is also important to teach *serving*. In fact, what better place might there be to learn it? Our children are familiar with a number of people over the years who have come to know Jesus Christ in our home. They understand that changed lives do not come through preaching sterile theology, but rather through learning to love people in practical ways.

Gordon and I have taught the principle of servanthood in the maintenance of our house, first of all. That principle started with simple jobs our children could do at the ages of three and four. We insisted that bedrooms be straightened out on a daily basis, clothes folded, the dishwasher emptied, and the dog fed. Certain hallways and rooms of the house were vacuumed by the children; trash was collected daily from all the wastebaskets. Those chores were done equally by both our son and our daughter. It was important, for example, for our son to understand—as his father believes—that there is no such thing as "women's work." It is all servant's work, and servants of Christ do it in order to serve one another.

I'd be dishonest if I conveyed the idea that our children have done all of that gladly. I will say that complaining has certainly been marginal in our home compared to what I hear about in many other families. One morning a few years ago Mark discovered that he was the only boy in the seventh grade who was doing the sort of things that he did before leaving for school, and he suggested the possibility that perhaps his parents were a bit unjust.

As I listened to his protestations, it occurred to me that his opinion was the result not only of what he'd learned about his peers, but also of my not having affirmed or thanked him for his work in the past weeks. We sat down together and I reminded him that because he did his chores, I was free to accomplish certain other things that he enjoyed me doing—such as my being in attendance when he played soccer. I shocked him by informing him that I really didn't love ironing, washing, and picking up either. The fact was, I said, that I did those things because I loved him and enjoyed serving him. Our conversation made a big difference in his attitude.

But servanthood is most exciting when the family enters a serving experience and shares in the fruits of accomplishment. I think something like that happened a couple of years ago when we decided to build Peace Ledge, our New Hampshire retreat.

In 1978 Gordon took a summer sabbatical leave. Along with the generous help of a friend who is a contractor, we decided to build a "retirement" home in New Hampshire. Whenever possible, the children were alongside of us, helping to build our saltbox home. One day a young man drove up from Boston to help us install the kitchen cabinets. Rather than make the long trip back and return the next day for a second day's work, he decided to stay overnight. We entertained him in our cabin nearby for lunch and supper. Almost immediately we noticed that he was in a very restless state. It wasn't long before he was sharing with us at the table some of the confusion in his life. Later after supper as he continued to talk with Gordon, Mark pulled me aside in the kitchen and said, "Mom, he's going to accept Christ if we give him a chance. Let's get out of Dad's way and see what happens."

Kristi, Mark, and I disappeared into the bedroom, knelt, and prayed for Dad and the young man who had come to our country cabin. It wasn't long before Mark cracked the door open a bit and listened. His face lit up. "Hey, God answered our prayers! The guy's asking Christ into his life right now."

And so he was. Later the children found a Bible they thought the cabinetmaker could use and presented it to him with their own note of Christian best wishes inside. The entire experience was a truly meaningful family exercise in servanthood.

You might call the pastor's home a difficult place to raise children, but I wouldn't trade the possibilities it presents since it gives us such varied and effective opportunities to demonstrate to our children what Christian living and ministry are all about. And servanthood is certainly one lesson easily learned in a pastor's home if the family members want to teach one another.

I was troubled one day when the son of a preacher we know said to my husband and me, "The only time I ever really hear my father speak is when he's behind the pulpit. At home he's a virtual recluse." A comment like that makes me realize how important it is to make sure that our home is a *place of warm communication*.

"Reach out and touch someone," the phone company advises. And in no place is that sort of thing more important than in the home of people in Christian leadership.

As in the marriage relationship, it's all too easy for parents and children to let their communication with one another fall into a state of disrepair. It is not enough to talk about events and people. Someone has said that most people talk about people and a few people talk about events. But, the observation went on, healthy and mature people talk about ideas, dreams, and visions and, might I add, matters of faith. We have made that final level of conversation a major ideal for communication in our family life.

It's hard work, I've discovered as a mother and a wife, to keep a family with teenagers together for meals. I'm alarmed that many homes have given up on that and permit each one to grab food for a meal as he or she can. A mother must often take the initiative when future schedules look destructive to family times. By planning ahead before we get into the middle of such busy periods, we can often avoid the drift or the conflict which may occur from a lack of communication.

I would be kidding if I tried to convince anyone that our mealtimes are always successful. Which of us in the Mac-Donald family has not brought a down mood to the table that everyone caught before the meal was over? Like every mother, I know the sickening feeling which comes when after having prepared a special meal in anticipation of the joy it would bring the family, I see a lovely experience collapse due to the uncooperative attitude of a family member.

Since I'm prone to generalize about one bad moment and think it to be a sign of total family disaster, my husband patiently reminds me that every home has an occasional negative encounter. And ours is no exception!

But for all the bad moments, there are certainly many good ones. We try to end many of our dinners with a time of reflection and devotions. If we've had problems during the meal, Gordon may suggest that we meet later after things have cooled off. There are many nights when either the schedule or the situation does not seem conducive to specific devotional exercises.

When we have periods of worship together, however, those are often rich moments for our family. Bible readings, a passage from a Christian book, and conversational prayer are usually part of our times together. Sometimes we may simply have an intense discussion that highlights a Christian value. Not infrequently, our prayers may be interrupted by impromptu laughter due to any number of gaffes or slips of the tongue. We've elected never to be overly disturbed by prayers or quiet moments which never make it to the "Amen." Perhaps, we reason, God enjoys laughter in our home just as much as we do.

Family traditions aid in communication. We've enjoyed reading a book together on a trip and have always attacked a jigsaw puzzle together during a school vacation. By the way, many of our completed jigsaw puzzles have been then pasted to a board, framed, and hung somewhere in our home as a reminder of family cooperation and shared memories. Other traditions include: pizza on almost every Saturday night; ice cream sundaes or popcorn after church on Sunday nights; family basketball games in which mother is allowed to play dirty; and an automatic stopover at Dunkin' Donuts each time we travel to our retreat in New Hampshire from our home in Lexington, Massachusetts.

Communication takes work. You also never know when an opportunity for it will occur. Recently, Mark and one of his friends joined Gordon in the woods for a day of cutting timber for next winter's firewood. A dull chainsaw blade became the center of their attention. As Gordon taught the two boys how to sharpen the chainsaw cutters, it became a perfect moment for showing how a dull saw can cause needless work and waste precious time. He observed that a dull inner spirit, impervious to the voice of God, can cause a young man to waste a lot of time making mistakes and reaping consequences he shouldn't have had to face. Call such moments in the woods "teachable moments," and take advantage of them whenever they arise.

Conflicts and misunderstandings are always a part of all relationships. They simply cannot be avoided. If they are, it is usually a sign that something is seriously wrong with the communication. The critical question is not whether conflict should exist in a family, but rather how it will be resolved. Conflict always creates a delicate moment in relationships; it has to be dealt with wisely. We have seen the effects on children when a father or a mother leaves a home after an unresolved verbal brawl and goes to minister in the congregation. I'm personally convinced that unresolved conflict under those conditions will quickly cause children to develop a cynical attitude about the nature of Christian faith.

Our children were quite small when we were visited by the well-known musical family, The Singing Murks, who gave a concert for our church family. The parents and their five children, traveling continually in a large bus, still maintained a closeness (not only geographically) that simply amazed us. The children obviously enjoyed one another. When asked about their tastes in young men, the girls all remarked that someday they'd like to marry men just like their brother and their father.

Naturally Gordon and I were curious about how this family intimacy had been created in the midst of a public lifestyle. Mrs. Murk shared with me that getting along had always been a top priority in her teaching of the children when they were small. If she found them to be in conflict, she would get them to look one another in the eye and quote Ephesians 4:32:

Be kind to one another, tenderhearted, forgiving one another, as God in Christ forgave you.

They were then to hug one another and say, "I'm sorry; I was wrong." Mrs. Murk insisted that she would accept nothing less than that wholesome formula.

The Murk children became expert peacemakers among themselves and among their friends at school. Our family was so impressed by what they taught us that we resolved to make it work in our home. And indeed it *has* worked.

There have been occasions when our family has driven together on the way to church, totally out of sorts with each other. Someone didn't wake up on time and made us all late as a result. Last-minute problems can create an air of irritability. Also, someone, usually Dad, may be extremely tense about an intricate plan that has to be followed through. More than once we have realized on the way to church that someone has to resolve the conflict. We have then pulled over to the side of the road, looked at each other, and said, "I'm sorry; I was wrong." It was important for all of us to be in fellowship with one another before we entered the house of the Lord and began to commune with other believers.

In the biography of Samuel Shoemaker, his daughter writes a touching tribute to her father. She acknowledges that her father never reacted to her; instead he always acted toward her needs. She wrote, "I caught his faith and find myself wanting to give it away as he did."[1]

If we would teach our children to apologize and to forgive, we must learn to do it ourselves. I have often found that hard to do since, in my younger years, I equated an admission of being wrong with weakness. Little by little I've learned the importance of being broken before the Lord and before my family. When I make a mistake, my children need to hear me admit that I've been wrong and need their forgiveness. And in acknowledging my weakness before them in a tender moment such as that, I am able to show them that I am also in the process of Christian maturing—just as they are. I want them to know that I am a real person, not a plastic one. Real people make many mistakes.

One of the great bonuses of being in a pastor's home is the opportunity to meet people. Since our home does not have a guest room as some homes do, it has been traditional that when a guest comes to visit, one of our children usually vacates his or her room and moves to the basement.

I am not aware that that has ever caused resentment since most of our visitors have gone out of their way to express gratitude to our children. There have been special times when persons of great repute in the Christian world have joined our table for dinner and our children have had the chance to get to know them. Such times have given our children the chance to see godliness up close and not simply behind the pulpit.

Perhaps no one person has made more of an impression upon our children than Dr. John Stott. He has always made it a point to greet our children personally by name and with an embrace. Several years ago when he occupied Mark's room for a few nights, he sent him a letter from England which in part read:

Dear Mark,

Many thanks for the use of your room as a place to both sleep and study. I shall remember you as my good friend and keep you in my prayers.

Yours,
Uncle John

That letter remained on our son's bulletin board for a long time. And when Mark has heard others speak of John Stott, he has enjoyed the quiet satisfaction that the great English rector and preacher is his friend. One grows under such circumstances and a pastor's home makes that kind of opportunity possible.

In studying the book of John, I was once struck with the

phrase "the disciples remembered." Such remembering occurs only when information has been both taught and heard during earlier teachable moments. Years later when the disciples faced unprecedented challenges, they were able to look back and remember the things the Lord Jesus had taught them through his words and his own example. They knew exactly how to act as a result. There were very few surprises.

That is exactly what we have tried to do as we have raised a couple of PK's in our home. We want them to store away memories so that someday they can draw upon them when they are on their own and have to face the moral and spiritual decisions from which no one is forever protected. We're hoping that they will remember moments in our home when they saw us serving hurting people. We're trusting that they'll remember how we stayed close to them when they were defeated or felt rejected by someone in their own world. We're anxious for them to remember particular patterns of response, insights, answers, affirmations, and convictions discovered in our home and applicable to their own future. In short, we can only pray that our kids have seen Christ in our home and that they, too, will "remember" when the time comes for them to accept responsibility for all of their actions.

When John wrote to Gaius, he said:

> *No greater joy can I have than this, to hear that my children follow the truth.* (3 John 1:4)

He, of course, referred to spiritual children, but I do not hesitate to claim the same words for Mark and Kristi whom the Lord gave Gordon and me. They are our number one ministry, and our life before them is definitely the Lord's work.

Part Two

INTRODUCTION

WHEN the Apostle Paul contemplated a visit to the Christian congregation at Rome, he wrote the people a remarkable letter, which has been preserved in the New Testament. In the introduction, he shared his anticipation of being with his people. He hoped to share "some spiritual gift" which would bring strength to the Roman Christians. But, he added, he assumed that there would be reciprocity. He expected that he would also be uplifted and refreshed by being a part of their fellowship.

On another occasion, Paul wrote of being comforted by the greetings and good news Titus brought to him from the Thessalonian congregation. In a third letter he acknowledged that he was deeply impressed by the faithfulness of the Philippian Christians who had sent him money, words of affection, and concern through Epaphroditus. Another poignant moment for Paul was toward the end of an arduous journey to Rome years later when he was under military arrest; Christians met him on the road to Rome and

> *on seeing them Paul thanked God and took courage.* (Acts 28:15)

I understand what Paul was saying and experiencing in those bits of Scripture. Having been part of three congregations, I know what it is like to be both the *giver* and the *receiver*. Like Paul, Gordon and I can look to three special groups of people who over the past years have played a great part in our lives. In each case we grew to love them and in turn felt deeply loved by them.

Environments of that sort help people to grow, and I think I can safely say that Gordon and I have indeed grown as persons, as Christians, and as a married couple. It would be difficult for me to calculate who did the most for whom. Have we given more to our congregations, or have they given more to us?

In previous chapters, I've written about several different "worlds" of my own: my inner walk with God, my self-awareness, my marriage, and my family. Now I must share one more "world," the one which is most public: the three congregations God has permitted Gordon and me to serve.

These congregations have been unique—each set in a different cultural context. And to some extent, each has drawn from us a slightly different response. Each place has forced us to face new experiences and new growth. I can now see the finger of God tracing the outline of the path for us to follow. So far it's been a great trip, and the mutual opportunities for maturing have been incredible.

Now let me take you on a cross-country tour from Kansas to Illinois to Massachusetts. In visiting the three congregations, you will encounter the process of a young couple entering ministry with enormous enthusiasm, if not much wisdom. Hopefully, you'll get a taste of some of the things which happen when two people set forth to do their very best. The "best" has rarely been attained, but Gordon and I have definitely learned much in our pursuit of it!

1
Sainty

Men are lonely because they build walls instead of bridges.
Anonymous

ST. FRANCIS is a Kansas farming community which sits astride U. S. Route 36 in the extreme northwest corner of the state. Twenty miles to the north and west of St. Francis —hardly a mile from the Colorado border—is a farming area known as Clough (pronounced clue) Valley. If there is a valley, I never saw it. And the fact that the area has a name does not indicate that there is any store, post office, streetlight, or even a concentration of homes. In fact there are none.

The Clough Valley Baptist Church, seven miles north of the nearest paved road with almost a mile between it and the nearest farmhouse, sits at the crossing of two section roads. Section roads, each a mile apart, make the countryside look like a checkerboard from the air. Into each of those squares the Kansas farmers sow winter wheat every September.

Across the road from the small brick church is a parsonage, an old remodeled farm home with the familiar windmill out back and a small patch of ground for the minister's garden.

If we had listened to the feelings and the counsel of most of our friends, I suspect we would never have noticed or heard of Clough Valley. Almost everyone we knew felt strongly that seminary days were a time of giving full attention to studies and only minimal attention to other forms of activity. Neither Gordon nor I believed that! He was a young man anxious to get preaching experience, and I was very concerned that he get it. Thus, we availed ourselves of every opportunity for him to speak.

Originally that priority had meant our having to drive hundreds of miles if a church in Wyoming or Nebraska asked Gordon to speak at a youth meeting, a Sunday school rally, or a public service. Again and again we would be thrilled and thankful if even fifty people were present when Gordon opened the Bible and preached one of a number of sermons in his growing file of messages.

It was that pursuit of preaching experience that brought us to Clough Valley one Sunday morning. The friendly farming families of that area had lost their pastor and in pursuit of a pulpit replacement had invited my husband to fill the pulpit. When the Sunday morning service ended, the people entertained us at one of the nearby farms with the typically delicious cooking that farm wives are known for. Incredible! When we left that tiny church the next Monday morning, we had been entranced by the simple but determined lifestyle of people who worked desperately hard to make a living from the soil.

It was more than a one-time visit, however, because a call soon came to our home in Denver, asking if we would consider candidating for the pastorate at the Clough Valley church. Gordon was in his second year of seminary, but it didn't take either of us long to make up our minds. Within a couple of months Gordon was pastoring his first congregation in "Sainty," the name given to the area by its natives.

Our first child, Mark, was only ten days old when we began our ministry at the little church 176 miles east of Denver. Moving into the parsonage across the road, we commenced a style of life that seems unbelievable and almost impossible when I look back at it almost twenty years later.

The schedule hardly varied for two years. Each Tuesday morning at 4:00 A.M. Gordon would climb into our little Volkswagon and begin a three-hour drive against the prevailing headwinds and tumbleweed of the Colorado prairie. Arriving in Denver by 7:00 A.M., he would attend a full four days of school and return to us by suppertime on Friday.

In these surroundings I faced the first great lesson that a woman has to grasp if she is to be effective as a Christian woman, a wife, and a mother: Submit to the fact that *God is in control of every circumstance.* I had a choice to make, and it had to be made quickly. I could enter each circumstance of my life, anticipated or unanticipated, and draw strength from the Lord and character lessons from the experience. Alternatively I could let the circumstances at Clough Valley make me resentful and restless, which they could easily have done.

The former alternative would make me into a fully useful person for God, while the latter alternative would make me into a very bitter woman who had to be carried and coddled and who would ultimately become an obstacle to her husband's life and ministry. I chose—as best I could—the first of the two choices.

The test of my choice came quickly. Mark was only a few weeks old when he came down with a serious intestinal infection. He and I were alone on the Kansas prairie in our new parsonage. I could see that his fever was rising to a dangerous level, and the result was an increasingly dehydrated condition. What aggravated the situation even more was the fact that I had no transportation, was twenty miles from the nearest town, and knew no local physician.

I remember stopping for a moment to think through the situation I faced. I was going to have to draw strength from God and help from some people I hardly knew. It came to me rather quickly that the Clough Valley people would be watching my performance quite closely. Having already lived under similar austere conditions for years, they were most unlikely to panic. Thus, if I had the slightest twinge of anxiety, it would be obvious to them.

Even though this was my first crisis with my first child, I somehow became aware that I might be setting a pattern of response to all sorts of unknown and critical experiences that would face me as long as I was married to a man in Christian leadership. People would come to know, as they went through this sort of thing with me, that I did indeed find my help in the Lord. He would have to give me a genuine sense of calmness and serenity. If I could not reflect those qualities, how could the congregation at Clough Valley really believe anything that Gordon would later say about the subject of faith from the pulpit? With the Lord's help, I passed the test.

A couple of months later Mark again became the instrument for a similar test. Riding about our small farmhouse in his walker, he had apparently decided to see whether he could descend the cellar steps. He couldn't! In fact, rather than walk down those steps in his walker, he somersaulted the length of the stairway and landed on cold, hard cement. The hematoma on the top of his head chilled my spine, but help came again. And I learned a second time that God could be in control of *every circumstance*.

On both occasions, the people of the congregation began to see that I could roll with the punches and not disintegrate under pressure. At the same time I began to realize that incidents of that sort, and even worse ones, were a part of their own daily lives. They could handle those things in stride, and I learned from them how to let everything be turned over into the hands of the God who lets nothing get out of control.

If I thought I was alone in the parsonage when Gordon was gone, I was wrong. Before the first winter had fully set in, I discovered that mice felt free to enjoy pastoral hospitality. One week alone, my journals indicate, I killed six of the little visitors. I confess that mice have a somewhat disturbing effect upon me, and my feeling of antipathy was accelerated one night when I walked into our bathroom during Mark's 4:00 A.M. feeding only to find one of them in our bathtub.

The mouse and I had a grand match to the end. It was quick with its feet, while I, quick with a broom, swung wildly as it attempted to climb up the slippery sides of the tub. I remember physically shaking from the violence and the strange fear I had throughout the episode. But again, I knew God was in control and he reminded me that there was something to be learned even in moments like that one.

In subsequent years, having been given the privilege of traveling abroad and having seen firsthand the sorts of things that missionaries face on a daily basis, my bout with the mice seems a somewhat tame affair, although at the time it certainly didn't seem that way.

If one comes to believe that God is indeed in control of all circumstances, the result is a growing sense of flexibility in trouble-filled moments. The Apostle Paul often talked about contentment under all circumstances; he also mentioned that in addition to contentment one should be thankful for everything that happens. Was that possible during a cold, blustery Kansas winter when I was alone and the windmill froze? At that moment flexibility meant calling a farmer's wife down the road and asking for instructions on how to unfreeze a windmill. I quickly learned the routine and went out to do it, finding myself having to repeat that on a regular basis. It didn't take long for me to become an expert in unfreezing frozen windmills!

Windmills do not freeze in a Kansas summer, but rattlesnakes appear in Clough Valley as soon as the snow disappears. Being thankful for them and maintaining composure in their presence became serious tests of my will. We killed more than one rattler on the church steps, and they died regularly under the wheels of our car. One day a large one slithered into our front yard where Mark and another small child were playing while we mothers were meeting for a missionary circle. I watched a brave woman from our group calmly grab a hoe and kill the snake.

"Do you ever worry about letting your children play outdoors when there are so many snakes around?" I asked her.

"You could worry about a lot of things," she said, "but a Christian has to put his or her children in the hands of the Lord and believe that the little ones are never out of God's sight. But of course we're always keeping a wary eye on things," she added.

I sensed that was another special moment when those wonderful people were teaching me something important for me to carry for the rest of my life: *When you really believe that God is in control of everything, then worry, panic, and resentment have no place in your life.*

If I needed any proof of that, it came when Gordon and I saw farmers plant (they called it "drilling") wheat. They waited for it to grow under the winter snows, saw it grow in the spring sun, and then faced the threat of June hailstorms when the vulnerable golden wheat was just about to be harvested. Each year the hailstorms seemed inevitable. Someone in the congregation would get "hailed out" by the random storms that could suddenly cross the afternoon sky, destroy one crop, and leave another crop untouched across the road.

We never saw a farmer panic under such conditions. But we did see more than one farmer plow a destroyed crop back under the soil and trust God for another better year. By nature Gordon and I tend to be "blitzers," people who run on enthusiasm and vision. Those farmers were "plodders," teaching us the value of living in a world which is bigger than any of us. Without realizing it, they had begun to show us that there are moments when we cannot control everything, that we must entrust ourselves "to the One who judges righteously." We quickly realized that if we opened our eyes, our ears, and our hearts, the people of Clough Valley would have much to teach us in their own quiet way. We became very conscious of the importance of listening and learning.

I also learned flexibility in our church services. Most mornings I played the piano during worship. At the rear of the church was a small "cry" room with cribs for Mark and other infants. If he began to cry while I was up front participating in the service, it was perfectly natural for me, as a nursing mother, to leave the front row for a matter of higher priority. That was life, and no one seemed to be offended or startled by it. I instinctively felt embarrassed, but no one else was. And so, I slowly learned to respond to matters in a more flexible way.

Recognizing and believing that God is in control of events also meant that I had to *learn how to receive* from the people of Clough Valley. I don't think I realized then that a significant factor in effective ministry is knowing how to receive from people. We had assumed that ministry meant only giving; no one had ever talked to us about receiving. But here I was surrounded by people who were often giving to our family in ways which seemed to be measurably more than we thought we were giving to them.

For example, they gave when it came to supplying us with food. A family would butcher a steer; then someone would stop by with some steaks, hamburger meat, and a roast or two. A garden would yield fresh vegetables. Some of the ears of corn, the tomatoes, and the cucumbers would make their way to our table. We regularly received two to three dozen eggs (complete with chicken droppings and feathers still attached) each Sunday. I think we ate better then than we have ever eaten in our subsequent years of ministry!

We received when it came to being taught a new way of life. Remember, Gordon and I are city people. Many of our city ways were a source of amusement to the folk at Clough Valley. They had a different sense of what was really important. Thus, like missionaries, we had to acculturate, taking on their ways, not grudgingly but lovingly. Thus it became important for us to watch, to listen, to ask questions. I learned new gardening and canning techniques; I learned how to go to farm auctions and buy secondhand things which we could use in our family.

We learned how to share clothes. People did not have garage sales at Clough Valley. What God had given them, they gave to one another when they had ceased to use them. All of us in the MacDonald family learned how to accept gifts of used clothing and to wear them with grace and appreciation. A five-year-old once said, "All of my clothes have had someone else in them." That was certainly true of our family's wardrobe!

The farming families of Clough Valley also taught me to take pride in making the paycheck stretch. I found myself becoming the woman in Proverbs 31 who "considers a field and buys it."

To the uninitiated, receiving can be misunderstood in at least two ways. *There are those who resist receiving, thinking it to be demeaning.* Their pride is hurt. They perhaps have not realized that while it may indeed be better to give than to receive, it doesn't mean that it is ever wrong to receive. Gordon and I learned that part of the completion of the loop of ministry was found in letting people minister to us when either we needed to receive or they needed to give. Furthermore, to receive from them meant that we loved what they had to offer and how they offered it. Had we been too proud to receive, we would not have been loving them, and that would have short-circuited the promised provision of the Lord.

A second misunderstanding is the exact opposite: *There are those who think that life is nothing but receiving.* We have watched some men and women in ministry who were far more attracted to what they were getting out of it than what they were putting into it. Gordon and I are increasingly concerned for the younger generation of people training for, and entering into, Christian service. We hear a great deal of talk centering on security for one's career, guaranteed salary packages, and demands for better and more comfortable situations. Both of us are convinced that the effectiveness of ministry is drastically curtailed the minute people get the impression that someone is in it for the money or for another kind of gain. Gordon and I are God's responsibility. Our policy has been never to ask what a salary will be, and his provision through his people has never let us down.

People who do not know how to receive usually do not know how to be thankful. How important to learn early in the years of ministry the varying ways of letting people know how grateful we are for what they're doing for the Lord and for us!

A colleague of my husband has just bought a home in need of much repair. Many of our church families have pitched in to help in the painting, rewiring, and carpentry work necessary to outfit the home for comfortable living. One of our elders, a painting contractor, took several of his employees into the house and in one day stripped the interior of old wallpaper, patched up the plaster, washed the ceilings, and did most of the painting. Why? The answer is simple. A few years ago the young pastor and his wife had given much affection and attention to that elder's daughter. You could say that the loop of ministry was now being completed. Because a young couple had given themselves freely a few years earlier, they were now on the receiving end in a very substantial way.

We learned other things in Sainty country: the importance of *building bridges instead of walls*. We realized that we had to learn what was important to these people. How else could we be all things to all people in order that we "might win some," as the Apostle Paul had said?

Lyndon Johnson and Barry Goldwater ran against each other for the presidency while we lived in Sainty. Many seminary students had Johnson stickers on their car bumpers. We were grateful that Gordon's father happened to be visiting us at the time just as Gordon was preparing to announce his own political affections via an LBJ sticker. Cheyenne County, Kansas, was Goldwater country, and we were probably the only people in our region who supported the Democratic ticket.

"Is this an issue that you're prepared to alienate people on?" Gordon's father asked. "If people are going to turn against you, is this the issue you want it to be predicated upon?"

The "youth" in us wanted to cry out that we had our rights to speak out on political matters. But my father-in-law's insight on that point was wiser than ours. He was helping us to understand that a pastor and his wife have to carefully evaluate each thing they present before their people. One must indeed pay the price of a conviction, but "before you go to the wall," Gordon now tells students, "make sure that this is the issue you're ready to die for. Make sure this is the largest possible issue."

That principle also extended to the way I dressed in Sainty. The farm people were by no means prudes, but their standards of taste and decency were a bit different from those that we had known in the large city of Denver. In those days hemlines were climbing ridiculous heights above women's knees, and many of the young wives of seminary students found it very easy to go along with the trend. But I soon realized that those hemlines would have needlessly offended the men and the women whom my husband and I were trying to love in the name of the Lord. Dress styles were not a big enough issue for which to "go to the wall." There were other things that were far more important, and we wanted to build bridges that would help reach the people whom we loved so dearly.

We have heard about and seen pastors and missionaries who took different positions on everything, demanding their rights on every occasion. We have seen them gain their rights and take their positions. And in most cases we have seen them lose the people whom they were called to serve. There is obviously a thin line between bridge building and total capitulation to the whims of people—only wisdom can draw that line. But in looking back, I can now see that whenever there was a conflict in Sainty, it was over the large spiritual issues that should concern a church.

Gordon and I learned that bridge building ought to be a factor in virtually every decision we make about our life-style. To this day what we learned in Sainty has meant that we dress in clothes that are tasteful but not attention getting. It has meant that we have chosen a quality of living in our choice of cars, furniture, and decor which meets the standards of our people but does not exceed them. If people want to break away from our church or us, let it be only for an issue of supreme importance, not because they are jealous of our possessions or our appearance.

I remember one day when we visited the lovely home of a friend in Denver. Our toddler, Mark, began taking awkward steps in various directions. Both Gordon and I were very aware that the woman hardly heard a word we were saying because she was so anxious that Mark might hurt or scratch her exquisite furniture. It apparently made little difference to her that I was ready to spring up to discourage him at a second's notice.

When we left the house, Gordon and I discussed the importance of never having a thing in our home that we were worried about losing through the mistreatment of a visitor.

The importance of the decision was reinforced the day that Mark etched a contemporary design in our own coffee table with his toy truck. Naturally, I was horrified, but my feelings were checked when I remembered that I had already pledged myself not to feel angry if someone else's child did that kind of thing. Why not the same treatment for my own? Besides, I thought, the Apostle Peter had told us that it was all going to burn up someday anyway and the important thing was to center in on *what kind of people we are*. In that case the issue concerned the kind of mother I was going to be for my son.

And so there in Sainty, I resolved that everything we

owned would be a tool and nothing more. For others who came to visit, our possessions would be tools of hospitality. For us, they would simply be tools of convenience. Things would not matter; *people* would. And while we've taught our children to respect the property of others, I cannot think of anything that we presently own that I wouldn't be willing to part with without an argument.

Thomas à Kempis' words ring true: "Do not seek to have what may be a hindrance to you and may deprive you of inward liberty."[1] Perhaps that is why parsonage living has never bothered me. We have been able to hold a parsonage loosely in Sainty and in other places that we have lived since. The parsonages simply have not belonged to us; they have always been on loan. We have been able to part with them without too much emotion when the Lord has called us to a different place. There's a slogan which makes a lot of sense to me: "In ministry use things; love people; never the opposite."

Learning how to adapt to people has meant *ministering to them where they are*. I said that Gordon and I are enthusiasts who like change. Well, change comes slowly in rural communities, especially in a place like Sainty. People there have known each other since birth. And when you see the same people every day of the week, there is less likelihood of dramatic changes in matters spiritual and otherwise. We discovered that people in Sainty had a hard time believing in the possibility of each other's changing. In many cases they were like a large extended family; it is hard to perceive change in such surroundings, let alone experience it.

It would have been pastoral suicide for Gordon to have preached and pushed people to show strong changes of direction overnight. I would have lost credibility with women had I pushed them too hard. Thus we learned to accept their slow manner of spiritual travel, which was capable of slight curves but rarely ready for the sharp, angular turns that we young people thought were so necessary.

We learned to *build bridges in the face of death*. In the space of six short months, our tiny congregation on the prairie faced the sudden deaths of two young people—one in a motorcycle accident, the other when a rattler spooked a horse which then trampled its rider.

In both cases the grief and the horror of the accidents were overwhelming. Here we were in our early twenties attempting to give leadership and spiritual stability to people who were twice our age and more. We had no experience from the past upon which to draw. We could only love the people and stand by them. Gordon and I discovered that *presence is far more important than words*.

We watched the rural culture express its grief when the farmers came and dug the graves together. At the end of the funeral services we watched them form double lines from the church sanctuary to the cemetery, standing silently as the grieving families walked between them to the open holes in the ground. We saw the men each take the shovel in turn and pour dirt on the lowered caskets. And finally we watched people weep and reminisce. We learned and loved by simply being there. As always we were able to observe the certainty of the faith of the farming families that expected God to use even the tragedies of life for the good.

We found that children can be bridge builders for a pastor's family. Clough Valley was made up of many older couples, and babies were in short supply. As a result, the people loved Mark, and he responded to them. I guess we learned to drag him along to about everything that ever happened. All he knew from the earliest days was being with loving people. That also meant that he was able to learn flexibility by being in different homes regularly and by being held in the arms of many different types of people.

One evening we visited the mud-brick home of a family of ten. The eight children had been raised by their father because the mother had been institutionalized after the birth of the last child. The father, Ben Trembley, was a deacon in our congregation and had become one of the most cherished people we'd come to know. His gentle spirit in the face of adversity was extraordinary, and his children grew in turn to be men and women who loved Christ. Gordon had the opportunity of baptizing his first son-in-law after introducing him to Jesus. To this day we prize an old rocking chair that Ben Trembley was going to discard because it had fallen apart. When we left Clough Valley, we took the pieces. One day when I was in a "reclaiming mood," we restored it. Today it stands as a testimony to our dear friend Ben.

Ben Trembley taught us that the wealthiest people in the church are not necessarily those who have money but rather those who have the Spirit. Ben never had a discouraging word. His face always had a smile when he climbed out of his dilapidated International Harvester pickup truck. He was usually the first to arrive for any service.

We, in turn, taught our farmers a thing or two about how to laugh. Not that they had to wait until we arrived to learn that, but their lives were often so serious and intense that they had a difficult time relaxing and enjoying one another. One evening we took all the couples thirty miles away to Wray, Colorado, where we'd reserved the back room of the Wray Cafe. At the end of the meal, Gordon suddenly passed a soup spoon around the enormous table. He asked each person to put a small crumb of food on the spoon and then pass it to the next person. The instructions were simple. The person holding the spoon had to eat everything on it when something dropped off. The tension rose as those gnarled farming hands began passing the spoon from person to person. Then the natural laughter erupted when someone had to eat the incredible combinations of food piled high upon the soup spoon.

It was in Sainty that we learned another important lesson. You could call it simply the lesson of *vision*. Today Gordon and I serve a relatively large congregation and have enjoyed opportunities to give spiritual leadership at a much broader level. Sometimes younger pastors will confess that they envy our present situation because their worlds are so much smaller and the people they serve do not seem to be interested in going anywhere in terms of growth and expansion.

I suspect that Gordon and I once had many of those same feelings. It was not because we didn't love and appreciate the people of Clough Valley, but because no one we knew outside of that area had ever heard of Sainty or the Clough Valley Baptist Church. After all, how much of the world could one change when church attendance hardly surpassed thirty-five or forty?

There were certainly those moments when both Gordon and I looked at others who had the so-called "great opportunities" in ministry, and we were tempted to be just a bit jealous. In our youthful enthusiasm to be effective, we needed to learn how to be content with where we were.

Miriam, the sister of Moses, has often been a reminder to me of the necessity of keeping jealousy from ever gaining a foothold in my spirit. A secret dissatisfaction once possessed her heart, and she began to compare her "place" with that of Moses and of others. God's judgment upon Miriam was leprosy. Later she repented and admitted that she had sinned and had acted foolishly. The growth of the entire nation of Israel was stalemated until Miriam was restored. If God is sovereign, how can Gordon or I envy anyone else's success? Frankly, it was a battle that we had to fight in those days when our vision seemed so limited. Now we realize what younger couples go through, since we are a few years away from Sainty and its rural limitations.

Ralph Turnbull relates the story of the late F. B. Meyer and his struggle in this same area of spiritual ambition and competition. When Meyer first went to the Northfield Conference in Massachusetts, he attracted a large crowd of people who came to hear him preach. However, G. Campbell Morgan also went to Northfield and lured the people by his brilliant Bible studies. The result was that Meyer's crowd began to dwindle while Morgan's grew. Meyer confessed a tendency to envy as he ministered to the smaller group. "The only way I can conquer my feeling," he said, "is to pray for Morgan daily, which I do."[2] That was a lesson that Gordon and I have also had to learn.

One afternoon while walking down our long gravel road, Gordon was thinking about the future. The Lord seemed to be speaking to his heart, "Gordon, if you'll not be faithful over a little, I'll never trust you with much." When Gordon shared that insight with me, we discussed the importance of living for today, regardless of the dimensions of a circumstance. We determined to serve the people of Clough Valley as if we might be doing so for the rest of our lives.

God vindicated that new decision of ours by making it possible for us to hold a Bible study for high school young people in the nearby town of St. Francis. We'd agreed to meet with them on Monday mornings at 7:00 A.M. before the school day began. Two families offered their living rooms so that Gordon could teach the boys and I could teach the girls. Though relatively close geographically, the people of Sainty lived on central standard time, while the people of Clough Valley to the west lived on mountain standard time. That meant that since it was actually 6:00 A.M. our time when we met, we had to rise at 5:00 A.M. in order to be ready for those young people!

Each Monday morning we would drop Mark off at a local farm home, drive to Sainty, go through our Bible studies, and then return for breakfast and the day's chores. "Is it worth it?" we asked again and again.

Yes, we thought on the final Sunday before we left Clough Valley, but not because the kids in those Bible studies had presented us with a silver tray etched with their expression of thanksgiving. *Yes,* we thought several times when we subsequently met at least four who, out of the original twelve, had entered some form of full-time Christian service. We met one as a missionary in Europe years later when he walked out of a crowd at a conference where Gordon was speaking. Another went into the pastorate; a third into evangelism. And the initiative for that Christian service seems to have started in part from those Bible studies held so early on Monday mornings. We discovered that the world, even in a little town like St. Francis, could be affected.

When the Billy Graham Association produced its first major film, *The Restless Ones,* Gordon convinced a BGA representative to preview the film in Sainty. Not many people know it, but the people of Cheyenne County in Kansas were among the very first in the United States to see that film.

The local pastors formed a committee, and a layman Gordon had discipled became the chairman of the film crusade. Fifty people were trained as counselors. We prayed, raised money, rented the high school auditorium, and got the publicity out. For each of three nights the film was shown to a packed house of one thousand. Over fifty people came forward to profess faith in Christ. We often wonder whether having more counselors might have drawn more inquirers. Even to this day the people who organized that film crusade almost twenty years ago have held annual meetings for Christians to celebrate their faith and give witness to it.

This past week a friend wrote of her experience at a retreat house:

> A lot of energy went into being "present" to people. I have always had a bad habit of being more interested in, and worrying about, something out in the future. It causes me to miss a lot of "now moments."

My friend's words took me immediately back to Sainty where through impatience for the future, Gordon and I could have missed our own "now moments." As the years have passed, he and I have become increasingly aware of the importance of those first three years of ministry. What we learned has had incalculable value. How forgiving the congregation was when we made mistakes! They supported us when they saw God giving us new and wider dreams. How it stretched us to enter a culture so different from the one we'd left! If we could have a measure of success in Sáinty, we reasoned, we could get along anywhere.

The people of Clough Valley Baptist Church continue to be a viable congregation. Many of them still pray for us and keep in touch with us regularly. And though we're far from them in distance, in time, and to an extent even in culture, we love them dearly. They were the first big chapter in our lives of ministry and we grew because of them.

2
Learning to Love—Loving to Learn

Am I prisoner of people's expectations or liberated by Divine promises? Henri Nouwen

I CLEARLY remember that particular Wednesday night. The congregation in Collinsville, Illinois, was voting on whether to call Gordon to fill their pulpit. A thousand miles away, Gordon and I waited anxiously for that important phone call which would bear news of the outcome.

We desperately wanted the word to be positive because we had found a mutual receptivity during our weekend visit —what Baptists call "candidating."

As with Clough Valley, some of our friends advised us against the idea of going to Collinsville. They said that Gordon was young and too inexperienced. The church in Illinois, it was rumored, had been badly hurt by its previous experience with the pastor. There had been a split in the congregation, and the people had known some bitter moments. A few who knew the situation thought that perhaps the church needed an older, wiser man who could bring things together. On paper they were probably right.

When the phone call came, we were informed of the unanimous vote supporting Gordon. We soon found ourselves on our way to Collinsville, a suburban town in the East St. Louis area, to join the people of the First Baptist

Church. Gordon and I gave our preparation period a lot of prayer. I think, looking back, that it was then that the Lord laid a very important insight on our hearts—one which we could have easily overlooked.

It occurred to us in the light of the demoralized situation that we'd heard about, that the *people of Collinsville needed to be loved, not changed.* Any healthy Christian man or woman can give *agape* love. Today when I hear so many pastor's wives put themselves down as inadequate and untalented, I am reminded of this simple truth: Anyone—regardless of talent or gift—can love if she or he asks God for the power and the will.

Gordon and I decided we would love the people. That meant that Gordon would deliberately attempt not to alter anything significant in or out of the congregation for the first year or two of our life there. The congregation had been put down, told that it was no good, criticized, and carved up. If the people were going to get back on the track, a pastor would have to restore their belief in what God could do through them. We quickly realized that the first step of that restoration would have to be in their knowing that we believed in them as a congregation.

Upon our arrival we immediately began to let the congregation know how much we appreciated everything they had done to welcome us to town. The previous pastor, for example, had complained endlessly about the parsonage. To us, however, it was a mansion and we told the people so. We actually did think it was a mansion; I suspect that Gordon and I had never anticipated living in anything so fine.

Families brought us food, helped us get things unpacked and cleaned, and entertained us in their homes nightly for dinner. It wasn't hard to be appreciative because we were delighted. Slowly I began to realize that an expression of appreciation was something in which I could take the lead on behalf of both my husband and myself. He was naturally busy in the early stages of getting his pastoral ministry started and was therefore apt to forget many of the things that deserved recognition and affirmation. So I began to increase my output of notes, the giving of small gifts, and my usual verbal expressions of praise to people who genuinely deserved it. And I was not above giving Gordon an occasional list of people whom he might call, write, or publicly affirm for their service to the Lord or to us. I've come to believe that those are some of the special ways a wife can be of help to her husband in leadership.

The same can be said about remembering names. Collinsville was considerably larger than Clough Valley, and it was not a simple thing to remember everyone we began to meet in those first few weeks. But it occurred to us upon arriving in our new Mid-western home that one way we could soon convince the people that we loved them was to work hard at calling them by name.

Anyone in the business of serving or selling to people will agree that remembering a person's name will go a long way toward gaining his or her confidence. Thus we pursued what was for us the *discipline of learning people's names*. The results were striking. Several people were absolutely amazed when after the second and third time of our having met them in the church or somewhere in the community, we could call them by name.

In addition, I soon began to write down the birthdays of people in the church leadership. Names and dates were kept in a calendar book; on weekends Gordon and I would fill out cards with words of greeting and affirmation so that people would have a word from us on their special day.

Just the other day a family returned to our present congregation for a visit. They had been in another part of the country for several months. When they had lived in Lexington, they had been quite active. Fortunately, I had kept her name and birthday in my calendar book and had seen it just a day or two before. On that particular Sunday when the family entered church for a brief return visit, I walked up to the wife and said, "Jeanne, it's your birthday today. Happy birthday!" All of them were astonished and got the message quite clearly: *The MacDonalds care for us.*

Whenever I have spoken of the importance of remembering things like names and special days in people's lives, someone has commented, "But you're good at that sort of thing; I'm not." Frankly, don't you think that's an unacceptable excuse?

Of course there are some people who have a special facility for remembering names, but I am not one of them. Remembering names is simply a matter of discipline and hard work to keep them right at the front of consciousness. When I'm involved in an introduction, I make quite sure to hear the name that is given. When a name is one that might be hard to remember, I'll often ask for it to be repeated. I may even ask for it to be spelled.

Sometimes I'll ask about the name's national origin and what a given name may mean: "Did it come from a family background? Does it have biblical significance?" Questions of that type help me remember names; they are also another way of letting people know that we're interested in them.

Furthermore, when someone begins to talk about his name, he often begins to reveal things about himself which are valuable in our getting to know him better. What fascinating conversations have ensued when a person has been asked whether he's always enjoyed his name and whether he thinks it describes what he knows about himself.

An additional value of keeping a journal comes from recording the names of people met during the day. Many times I've returned to my journal to retrieve the names of children in a family so that when we wrote a note or sent a gift, we could include the smallest of the children in the greetings. Haven't you told people that you really love them when you remember even their children's names?

We also began to love the people by extending our hospitality. As soon as the house took on a reasonably ordered appearance, we held an open house. Most of the membership had not been in the parsonage for years. This was their chance to meet us as real people in the context of our home. I was eight months pregnant with our daughter-to-be, Kristi, but the help I recruited from several willing women in the church made hosting the open house an easy thing to do.

Later on we decided to use our home as a tool for a very ambitious hospitality project. Setting aside money in our budget and clearing every Thursday night for ten or twelve weeks, we set out to serve every adult member of First Baptist Church—thirty of them at a time. It could have been a gigantic project if not planned properly, and so we gave a lot of time to thinking through each step of the process.

Our objectives were multiple. Gordon and I wanted to know people better, of course. We wanted to serve them and more than that, we wanted to serve them *together*. Also we were hoping that people would be drawn to one another as a result of being in our home. Many of them had been hurt by broken relationships in the past, and they needed an experience of wholeness to heal past memories. How could it be done?

Having been to central Europe in recent months, we had learned about beef fondue. So we contacted eight or ten fondue pot owners and asked them if we could borrow their pots for three months. Then I recruited a couple of hard-working high school girls who would be willing to help me each week in the kitchen. Invitation lists were carefully drawn up. Every list included a wide spectrum of people in terms of age and level of faith commitment. Each family was phoned personally and asked to bring a pound of cubed sirloin.

When they came to our home on given Thursday nights, we assigned them to teams to play games that would evoke hilarious laughter. And when it was time to eat, our guests sat at tables in our dining room and living room and learned how to eat fondue. The very act of people sharing in part of the cooking helped draw laughter and animated conversation. All the while, Gordon and I went from table to table waiting on people, keeping their water glasses filled and their plates filled with different things to eat.

Later in the evening we asked the men to clear away the tables, and then we invited everyone to join a circle in the living room where people were asked to give answers to what has been traditionally known as the "Quaker Questions." In turn each person around the circle was asked, "Where were you in the seventh grade?" A strange query, to be sure, but one that tends to elicit some fascinating answers. The second time around the circle, people were asked, "What was the warmest spot in your childhood home?" Our guests suddenly came alive. Then the third and final question was "When in your life did you feel closest to God?" That always brought our evenings of hospitality to a beautiful conclusion as men and women unashamedly shared important moments of faith in their lives.

Many things happened during those wonderful evenings. Perhaps one of the most significant was that our congregation saw Gordon and me working together. We shared the load of serving. Many weren't used to seeing such "team work" in areas of responsibility once thought to be "wifely tasks." We quickly learned the power of a home where hearts are set on being hospitable. People often grow in their walk with Christ and one another when servanthood is mirrored in some way before them.

It was during those early months of entertainment in our new Collinsville home that I became more and more aware of the tremendous effect a ministry of hospitality can have on a congregation. * I have, as a result, become a student of those who obviously have what the Bible calls the "gift of hospitality." We've also experienced the acceptance and warmth in hospitality when, for example, we have been in

*Turn to the Appendix for specific suggestions on hospitality.

the home of our close friends Jud and Jan Carlberg. Jud is Dean of Gordon College and his wife, Jan, is the Director of Student Affairs. Our friendship with the Carlbergs goes back to seminary days, so we have had many years to reflect upon each other's spiritual growth.

Not long ago I was present when Dr. Carlberg addressed a group on some of the rich things he and his wife have learned about hospitality. I was deeply impressed by the difference between entertainment and hospitality; he said:

> Hospitality is a safe place; entertainment is a show place. Hospitality focuses on people; entertainment focuses on things. Hospitality creates an open atmosphere; entertainment can be neat and closed. Hospitality exudes a warm attitude; entertainment can degenerate to being cool and calculated. Hospitality puts one at ease; entertainment implies competition. Hospitality is a harborous disposition; entertainment sets up a win or lose attitude in which one is closed off to dust, dirt, and people. Hospitality involves making people feel good in God's world. God created a hospitable world; sin made the world inhospitable. By our supportive action, we can dispel the sinful atmosphere.

Given the rise in the cost of living in the past few years, I'm not sure that we could entertain today as extensively as we did a few years ago. Nevertheless, there are still ways that anyone can practice hospitality by sharing in food preparation. Looking back I realize how much those nights together each Thursday influenced our congregational life, adding a warmth and an acceptance in many people's hearts that would not have happened had we not developed such close contact.

When my husband and I take the time to watch a football game on TV, I am often fascinated by the slow motion replays that show exactly where a play went right or wrong. It occurs to me that there are things worth sharing almost on a slow motion basis that could be of help to other women, who like myself, find themselves in positions of leadership. Thus I want to be careful and deliberate in recalling this particular period of our pastoral experience because it demonstrates how one's strongest traits can also become one's most serious weakness.

It was during our Collinsville days that we began to *discover both the strengths and weaknesses of our leadership style*. I suppose that discovery was best seen in our lives in terms of the quality of our relationships. It was never difficult for Gordon and me to attract people to us, simply because, I suppose, we have always tried to be sensitive to people's dreams and struggles and because we have tried hard to affirm what we see people becoming and doing.

But what seems to be a very positive and enviable trait can also work to the detriment of people and a pastoral family. Frankly, we failed a number of people in our congregation because we never understood the importance of communicating to them the difference between relationships which are for the purpose of Christian growth and those relationships which are solely for the purpose of building a friendship. To put it another way, we did not realize that a pastor or any Christian leader has to face the fact that a congregation or any Christian organization is a social grouping which has many people—for varying reasons—who are desirous of being in the spotlight with the leaders. Since we didn't understand that at the time, we were prone to making several miscalculations about the best way to minister to people.

It was difficult for me to say no when people extended various invitations or requests in my direction. As the wife of a pastor I found myself wanting to please everyone. Now I realize that I probably had an underdeveloped part of my personality, which at that time needed to feel as if everyone liked me. Whatever the reason, my inability to make sound judgments about the use of my time and energy caused me

to enter quickly into a schedule of activities and relationships which could only be maintained because I was still
young enough and had the physical energy. I was touched
that other women wanted my advice, desired my presence
at their showers and parties, and sought me out to shop and
have lunch with them. At first I felt personal affirmation,
for the phone was constantly ringing with callers interested
in my opinions on various decisions they had to make.

Some probably didn't help the situation as they marveled
at my constant availability and what they called a "sweet
spirit." I guess I permitted them to believe, inadvertently,
that I had the capacity to live up to their growing expectations. But in fact I was getting up earlier, staying up later,
and probably, on many occasions, not giving myself the
adequate rest and refreshment to be all that my family
needed and wanted in a wife and a mother. But after all, as
we have all reasoned at one time or another, this is the
Lord's work and people have unending needs. . . .

I think it is important to say that there were many wonderful men and women in the Collinsville congregation
who never had anything to do with creating the situation
that I was getting myself into. But then again there were
some, as there will be in every congregation and social
grouping, who seem to be willing to draw endlessly upon
the resources of any leader who is ready to give. There are
those who seem problem prone because they go from one
crisis to another: marital struggles, loneliness, the inability
to resolve broken relationships, all sorts of physical and
emotional sicknesses, and mysterious and often indefinable
spiritual problems.

I often failed these types of people during the Collinsville
years because I permitted them to go on believing that I was
instantly available each time a personal crisis erupted.
Sometimes what they really needed was loving but firm
advice or admonition. Yet on the few occasions when I
tried to give that, it seemed to hurt. The feedback indicated
that I had apparently stopped loving them. Now I realize

that even that false conclusion was a defense mechanism which certain people unconsciously use to keep someone like me in their relational grip. I found myself involved in an increasing number of difficult encounters.

That kind of "grind" not only drains one's physical makeup, but also saps the inner spirit. One begins to feel as if nothing is ever enough. I compared my life with the needs of women around me and said, like the disciples who had a small boy's lunch, "But what is this among so many?" I began to live with an enormous sense of inadequacy and guilt.

Joan Jacobs, in her book *Feelings,* is absolutely correct when she says that we are often captured by a false sense of guilt. Such guilt really indicates an attitude toward ourselves. True guilt occurs when we've broken God's laws. False guilt erupts when we or others set up unattainable or superficial expectations of ourselves that even our Lord would not have attempted. Frankly, that's exactly what I was doing. I had the growing inner sense of being trapped. I was, in Henry Nouwen's words, "a prisoner of people's expectations, not liberated by the Divine promises."

The dilemma of those Collinsville days came to mind when a friend wrote to me recently:

> What do I do about people who hope that I will be their "best friend," confidante, in fact, almost their "Jesus"? These people have genuine, sometimes horrendous, needs, and yet, if I try to be their "Holy Spirit"—making judgments, asking questions, and giving advice—am I not also in danger? Some have homes which are chaotic, children who are neglected, meals which are unplanned and unprepared. Each one is perfectly willing to let *me* assume child care, housekeeping, etc., for them. In fact, I have actually had a person call, say she simply can't cope and won't I "please come and take over while she takes a breather?"

Many of us do not have the training which would help us to spot and to understand the nature of the person who tends to lean heavily on whomever is available. Often a person in a leadership role is pursued as a substitute for a parent with whom the weak person has had an unhealthy relationship. We can be pressed to provide the companionship or compassion which a spouse is not giving due to a below par marriage. A person who is not generating healthy relationships with peers will often flee to someone else who is available for caring and discipling.

It's possible to be suddenly surrounded by people who wish to draw strength, recognition, and affirmation, but who have little desire to mature to a point of self-sufficiency and have a servanthood life of their own.

I needed to learn how to say no to some people, and I did not do a very good job of it. The leader-listener who risks saying no will gently expose the empty talking and will instead spotlight the need for action. But we who are trying *only to please* often will not do that. We wrongfully assume that to love means always to conform to whatever someone says he thinks he needs or wants. Ironically, while we may think we have ministered and comforted, the truth is—in the long run—we probably have not. In fact, we may have succeeded in hurting marriages, families, or other relationships more deeply.

Those of us in leadership have to learn that to give acceptance and sympathy to only one person with one side of a story may be quite dangerous. We can thus become a person's excuse for not working on his part in a sour or ungodly behavior pattern. In some cases we may allow people to repeatedly gain from us the strength that should come only from God.

From the context of wisdom and experience, we can begin to learn that the answer lies in a balance of such things as: timely disengagement, speaking the truth in love, sensing where the whole story has yet to be told, and of course, knowing our own mental, spiritual, and physical limits. I've seen the overly dependent person come to important inner growth and later break the pattern of dependence. That sometimes occurs when someone helps him see his latent capabilities and his need to have realistic expectations. Sometimes it happens when a person helps the needy individual overcome the habit of manipulating people through pity and sympathy. Then on occasion, change may happen as the result of having introduced the person to someone with much greater needs than he himself had or thought he had.

I should also mention that now when someone needs counseling for a personal problem, I usually meet with the person *away* from my home. Doing that was impossible when the children were smaller, of course, and I had to be near them. Now, I'll usually meet women in a nearby restaurant, in the church parlor, or in my husband's office if he's elsewhere.

I've learned that it's easier for me to terminate a discussion when I feel it is necessary. Away from my home, I am free to excuse myself. In my own home, however, I have to wait until the other person feels ready to leave. Meeting elsewhere is not motivated out of a desire to manipulate another person. It's simply recognizing the fact that the counselor knows best when a conversation or counseling session has reached its point of maximum effectiveness. A "neutral" place makes that kind of closure possible.

In Collinsville I also learned about the second kind of person pastors and wives frequently encounter in any congregation. That's the one who simply enjoys the presence of people in leadership. I hasten to add that this kind of person is often genuine and very fine and also is enjoyable company. He does nice things in nice places, laughs a lot, and is often quite complimentary and agreeable about things that those of us in leadership do.

Unfortunately, something is always missing in exchanges with that kind of person. Often the person enjoys having fun but really does not seek to grow spiritually or to become interested in the kind of commitment required of a disciple of Jesus Christ.

Again, in our younger years neither my husband nor I were perceptive enough to understand the differences in people. We accepted every invitation extended to us; we joined every group that would have us. We were always pleasantly surprised at how effusive people were with their comments about what we were doing in church leadership. Frequently we heard statements of strong support about an idea or a program in which Gordon was interested. Not infrequently, however, on the long drive home from that type of encounter, both of us would admit that something had been missing. What was it?

After a year or two we discovered the missing link. The picture became clearer when we realized that we might have a delightful time with some groups, but the conversation and the activity had little or no connection with *spiritual* things. Slowly we became aware that we were sometimes invited to certain gatherings not because we were spiritual leaders but because we were the heads of a social grouping —the church—and perhaps because leaders were seen to be attractive and nice to have around.

What began to trouble us was that the people who possessed a genuine hunger for growing in Christlikeness were often crowded out of our social schedule. That is, of course, a generalization and there were many exceptions to what I'm describing. But in the early days of ministry we were not sensitive or wise enough to figure all of that out. And it cost us.

There were many times when Gordon and I simply had to back off from groups and relationships which were nonproductive in terms of our reason for coming to Collinsville. Somehow we had to get the fact across that we had come there for three basic purposes: to lead a movement of spiritually growing people, to care for genuinely struggling people, and to train earnestly committed people. Having fun would certainly be a part of such goals but not the main agenda. It's frightening to realize how easily one who enjoys being the center of attention and likes to be liked can be drawn away from the primary objectives of ministry.

The third relational lesson I had to learn was perhaps the most difficult and painful. It concerned the matter of training individuals and couples for spiritual maturity.

Gordon and I set out to engender relationships among some people whom we thought capable and eager for spiritual growth. However, it soon became apparent that we were making some basic mistakes. The chief error centered in our failure to communicate why we were pursuing the people we set out to know. Our concern as pastor and wife was to disciple them toward Christian maturity, but all too often others thought that we were pursuing a close and personal friendship.

On several occasions we invited groups of couples to come to our home for a Bible study for a period of six or eight weeks. When the time came to terminate our relationship so that we could disciple another group, we found that the first group seemed genuinely hurt. Much to our bewilderment we discovered that on a few occasions people actually became angry and hostile toward us because they assumed that we had simply "dropped" them as friends. We were shocked at such reactions especially because, like many others who are young in ministry, we had heard the success stories of spiritual leaders across America who discipled people and left behind a string of healthy Christians carrying on independently of the leader. The more we heard stories of that sort, the more depressed we became about our own inability to do the same thing.

Frankly the people we served were not the ones who failed—Gordon and I were. We had not been clear enough from the beginning in telling groups our intentions. Since those early days of feeling that we had failed a lot of people, my husband and I have learned to tell people at the very outset the purpose and the time frame of a relationship.

We've also given them a chance to decide whether they felt that kind of relationship was for them. We've learned to release people before an unhealthy dependency has been created.

Some readers may conclude that the life of a pastor and his wife is far too crowded with opportunities for disaster and error. That simply isn't true. Mistakes? Of course. But as I recall our days in Collinsville, the great moments and experiences almost completely blot out the instances of difficulty and stress. The people were lovable and we learned to love them. But as we taught them, they also taught us. And I think it's important to share some of the highly positive things which Gordon and I learned from the people of that congregation.

For one thing, we learned *how to be ministered to in some special ways.* Shortly after Kristi was born, I spent six weeks in bed with mononucleosis, becoming completely dependent upon my husband and several women in the congregation, who carried on my chores for me.

I learned in those weeks that almost any experience can be used to enhance one's personal growth. I remember that Gordon and I took some of our greatest marital strides forward during those weeks of my illness because we had time to talk without interruption. Occasionally in an afternoon he would sit on the edge of my bed, and we would share in-depth matters that had often been put on the shelf for want of better times to talk. I learned that even sickness can provide the opportunity of deepening a special relationship. In that light, I could hardly resent my being bedridden!

My sickness also gave me the chance to learn some special lessons about how and how not to help people. During that time, for example, I discovered that I should never call someone and ask, "What can I do?" and "Do you need anything for dinner?" Most people in a difficult strait like mine will probably answer that they really don't need anything—even if they actually do. The sick often feel that being sick is in itself an imposition.

Another thing I learned from those helpful church ladies is the wisdom of calling someone and saying, "I'm planning to bring supper for you and your family. Which night this week would be the best?" A direct and defined plan of action is far superior to some sort of innocuous question that leaves the burden of performance or response on the one who needs the help. I also discovered that taking meals in disposable containers eliminates the stacks of dishes and containers that have to be returned at a later date. That lesson alone seemed worth the price of my sickness!

In those younger years I often found it hard to let people do things for me. That perhaps came from a mixture of pride and the fear of imposing on anyone. But I gradually learned that that was a *very* unhealthy attitude for the wife of a pastor to have. I had to learn the pattern and the meaning of grateful receiving every bit as much as I'd had to learn the gracious way of giving.

In fact, *when we receive, we can often learn new and creative ways to give.* During a time of personal tragedy, a dear friend gave me a handful of envelopes marked with the days my family and I would be away during our time of grief. Every morning I was to open the appropriate envelope and find an encouraging note containing a word of Scripture and an affirmation of my ability to handle the sorrow of the situation. What a ministry! Not only was I deeply blessed by it, but I also learned to imitate my friend's thoughtful gesture. I've duplicated her effort scores of times since to help others needing encouragement. I doubt whether I would have ever thought of such an ingenious form of giving on my own, but that doesn't matter. Today I'm able to use it because when I was weak and needy, I was willing to be served by a friend.

Several years ago Helen Roseveare, a physician and missionary to Zaire, spoke at the great Urbana Missionary Convention. She shared the fact that she had often been disheartened by the serious illnesses that seemed to hit her without warning. After long bouts with cerebral malaria and hepatitis, she had begun wondering whether to return to England or to remain a burden to her fellow missionaries.

One day Helen was struck by the insight that *we all like to be needed.* For years she had been the only physician for approximately a half-million people. As such, she had been the one in demand, always on the giving end. The Africans, on the other hand, had always been on the receiving end— the ones having to say thank you. Now the roles had been reversed, and the Africans had come to know the fulfillment and the joy of being needed. Once the giver, she had now become the receiver. Now the patient, she had to be served by those whom she had originally served. They nursed, fed, and washed her. She, in turn, learned to say thank you.

Learning to be vulnerable and to receive the help of others in a congregation came as the outgrowth of our Collinsville experience. One day our three-and-a-half-year-old daughter, Kristi, was rushed to the hospital with a stomach full of turpentine which she had accidentally swallowed. We didn't know it at the time but she had been born without the sense of smell and thus was unaware that what she was actually raising to her lips—a milky white substance in a bowl—was turpentine, not milk.

The first twenty-four hours in the hospital were terrifying. The doctors had warned us of the possibility of kidney, lung, and even brain damage. They made no promises that Kristi would even survive the crisis. Gordon and I were like so many others we'd seen who had faced grim emergencies and had sat in the waiting room of the intensive care unit. Now Gordon couldn't march in and announce that he was a pastor visiting a patient. This time he was simply an ordinary person, restricted by the rule that parents could have only five minutes of visiting time every two hours.

As we sat helpless and wondering what the future might bring, we learned what would have been impossible to comprehend under any other circumstance: the sustaining power of prayer. We'd often been on the intercessory end of prayer for others; now we were on the other end. It was a Wednesday night; the church had gathered to pray for Kristi's recovery and normalcy. Knowing that they were back there on their knees before the Lord on our behalf was very comforting to us.

Many of Gordon's fellow pastors stopped by as we waited in the lounge. Some of the godly deacons from our church followed. Each one embraced us, prayed, and spoke the special words of Scripture and Christian affirmation. Our visitors brought peace, love, and assurance. Their very presence helped us to reaffirm that God was right there in the waiting room.

Later when we were alone, Gordon said, "No matter what happens to Kristi, this experience will be unforgettable for us. We've gone to the bottom of life and found that God is even there." That fact remains etched into our spirits, but it came to us because others presented themselves and ministered to us.

Kristi lived without any bad aftereffects. Today she is a healthy teenager who barely remembers what must have been a nightmare for her at the time. We, of course, remember it well, for through it we learned the meaning of being cared for by people who bring a word of grace and a message from the Lord. Also our perspective on the meaning of giving to people changed. Neither Gordon nor I would have ever grappled with such issues had we not first been reduced to helplessness in those early years of our ministry.

Things do not always work out as well as one would wish. In Collinsville our family had another lesson to learn: *how to perform in times of seeming defeat.* We came to realize that those of us in leadership mustn't complain or whine when things do not go according to the "script." Being "out in front," a leader can easily command sympathy and morbid attention. While it's important to share feelings occasionally, we've discovered that there's a time to keep hurt and sorrow and deep feelings to ourselves. Brigid Herman, a pastor's wife of many years, put it this way in a small devotional booklet:

> Sorrow may be among God's mightiest angels, but it does not necessarily, and in itself, do angels' work. A time of sorrow is often a time of moral and spiritual relaxation, of weakening self-pity, and of incontinent demands upon the sympathy of others. It breeds self-importance rather than heroism. And the selfishness of sorrow feeds upon speech. Small wonder that the masters of the spiritual life have always held up as the ideal what all writers used to call "the virginity of suffering"—the habit of keeping silence concerning our sorrows to all except God! There is of course a limit to such counsel.
>
> Human sympathy of the right kind is sacramental, and God comforts his servants, as he comforted St. Paul, "by the coming of Titus." But while past ages tend to deny the divine nature of sympathy and fellowship, our own tends to idolize them. We again and again weaken ourselves and others and miss the divine consolation, by running to this person and to that before we make our need known to God. In the joy of our discovery of the sacredness of human affection, we forget that it remains unshakably true that whatever be the power of human sympathy, the soul of man is created for direct, immediate communion with its God. Nothing, however lovely and true in its own order, can take the place of that immediate touch. And that touch will not be experienced by a soul that has exposed itself to every well-meaning hand, in its feverish search for comfort.[1]

Her words also apply to the times when a pastor and his

wife face criticism from people in the congregation. In-
volvement with people means that there are going to be
times when men and women with good or bad motives will
comment on things that are important to a leader, and their
statements will not always be pleasant.

Most pastoral experiences begin with a so-called "honeymoon" period between leader and the congregation. It
appears for a short while as if the honeymoon will go on
forever. But sooner or later the pastor discovers that not
everyone is always pleased with what he is doing. With that
discovery comes an important moment: handling the unpleasant feedback.

A. W. Tozer, the modern Christian mystic, once wrote
that the mark of a person of God was that he or she would
elect never to fight back when attacked for any reason. It's
a simple principle, but Gordon and I chose to adopt it at any
cost. We pledged to the Lord and to one another that we
would "fight back" only on those occasions when God's
truth had to be defended or the rights of others were being
jeopardized. *We would not knowingly ever defend ourselves.*

That's not an easy commitment, especially for a wife
who admires and feels defensive about her husband. I guess
I feel perfectly free to criticize Gordon when we are alone,
but I confess to bristling when I hear anyone else prepare
to do it. And that's important to remember because there
are people in a congregation—especially women—who'll
approach the wife of a pastor and attempt to use her to relay
messages and comments that they don't have the courage
to bring directly to the pastor. How did I deal with that sort
of thing?

First of all, I had to learn to listen to people like that and
offer no immediate self-defense. I quickly learned to allow
no one to use me as a conduit to my husband. If I sensed
that someone was trying to do that, I would immediately
direct her to talk to my husband.

Even if certain comments seemed unfair or reflected a

178

lack of appreciation, I learned to accept them and to ask myself whether there could be any truth to them. I must admit that there were times in those early Collinsville days when it was almost impossible for me to keep my mouth shut when someone spoke out of ignorance or from an improper motive. However, it was more important for me and Gordon to teach ourselves the art of draining every criticism of the tiniest element of truth.

We had to school ourselves to see things as others might be seeing them and thereby gain insight into their perspectives or frustrations. Learning to "contextualize" people's criticisms has made a great difference in our attitude toward the comments and the people. It's helped us see that there were times when what we had said or done was not exactly what people had heard or seen. We learned by listening.

When we were wrong, we tried to acknowledge it and express appreciation to the critic, especially if a person had come directly to Gordon to voice his or her concern. As people noticed that we could take criticism, they became willing to "level with" us. In that healthy atmosphere, *all* of us grew. My husband became surrounded by several godly men who were willing to be honest and open with him. They often saved him from disastrous mistakes.

Perhaps part of my role was to encourage Gordon to listen as carefully as possible. I wonder how many pastors' wives have failed their husbands at this point. A man in the public eye needs his wife to stand resolutely with him. But isn't she also the best one to encourage him to listen? Of course, the husband has to be willing to listen!

I've frequently seen men in leadership make serious mistakes in judgment—saying or doing immature things or reacting poorly to unpleasant situations. Why didn't their wives help them see how they were coming across to others? We wives needn't have all the answers for our husbands, but we can perhaps be perceptive enough to encourage them to pursue those who do. Over the years when I've felt that Gordon was struggling with an issue, I've often encouraged him to visit men in the church who could give him sound advice. Many times that was all he needed. As a result, both he and the church benefited!

Another thing I learned more about in Collinsville was forgiveness. It's an indispensable discipline in spiritual leadership. If one cannot learn both to give and to receive forgiveness, the effectiveness of a ministry will be quickly nullified.

The prayer of Christ on the cross:

> *Father, forgive them; for they know not what they do* (Luke 23:34)

became quite meaningful to me. It saved me from a lot of ill feelings toward people who had inadvertently hurt the congregation or my husband. My natural instinct had been to fight back, to embarrass the offender, or to reduce him or her to impotence by sharp words or vindictive actions. However, Gordon and I had begun to appreciate the better spiritual insight of assuming that people really didn't realize what they were doing. Starting with that principle saved us many needless confrontations or agonizing polemics.

It occurred to me that part of our role in ministry is *absorbing the anger of other people*. Those whom we'd been called to serve were often themselves the targets of experiences and frustrations in their daily lives over which they had no control. Sometimes they simply took their feelings out on the first person they met, especially if they sensed that the person would not fight back.

The Apostle Paul's awareness of his role among the Thessalonian believers greatly encouraged me. He saw himself as a nurse-comforter and a father-encourager. When a few people assume that sort of role, there can be healing and restorative love in a congregation. Strength is built and there is a chance for a new start, instead of the raising of walls and the cry of battle among people.

Slowly through the acts of forgiving and of absorbing anger, Gordon and I began to recognize that our role in relationships was often that of peacemaker. The world has enough warriors. It can certainly use a few more peacemakers.

I once read of Thaddeus Stevens, a Massachusetts congressman who bitterly wished to crush the South at the end of the Civil War. When he heard President Lincoln stress the importance of binding up the wounds of the nation—forgiving and reconciling—Stevens pounded the cabinet table and shouted, "Mr. Lincoln! I think enemies ought to be destroyed!"

Those present report that Lincoln quietly responded, "Mr. Stevens, do not I destroy my enemy when I make him my friend?"

That attitude is totally Christian and is the context in which people can grow to be more like Christ. Being agents in forgiveness and absorbers of people's anger and hurt became relational objectives that Gordon and I have continued to pursue.

We learned something else in Collinsville for which we will forever be grateful: *the pursuit of excellence.* Do not confuse excellence with perfectionism. Both of us know that we will never be perfect, but that does not deter us from pursuing excellence. We learned the principle of excellence from a number of sources: our reading, spiritual mentors, and our growing awareness of the effects of shabbiness in our work. It embarrassed us to see the King of Kings served halfheartedly or from a begrudging spirit.

Shouldn't sermons be preached to the maximum level of one's ability? Shouldn't music reach the highest possible standard? Shouldn't our quality of leadership in spiritual matters match the same intensity that people are used to seeing in the world of business, education, and government? Shouldn't all that we do be done to the glory of God; that is, in the spirit of biblical excellence?

We worked hard to pursue excellence in Collinsville,

along with the other two couples who joined us on the pastoral staff. All six of us wanted to give the congregation a model of how committed people could get along with each other. We wanted them to see it in our style of work, and we certainly wanted them to see it in our marriages and families. We pursued excellence not only in our general relationship and work, but also through the musical talents that we combined as we sang together. Our congregation saw us laughing with each other, praying with each other, serving and supporting one another. But perhaps they saw the quality of excellence most dramatically during our musical presentations.

Not long before our family left the congregation in Collinsville, I was invited to accompany a group from the congregation on a missionary tour of countries of the Caribbean. I was the group's "mascot," a role which provided me one of the most memorable experiences of my life. We visited three missionary enterprises of the Worldteam Mission in Haiti, the Dominican Republic, and Jamaica. As we traveled, we saw evidences of progressive Christian growth, culminating in the witness of the young people at the Jamaican Bible Institute.

On our final day in Jamaica, the young people of the school sang for us. Later in the evening when I was alone, I wrote in my journal:

> Today the Holy Spirit broke me through the simple yet profound manner of a woman. A woman whose fingers were God's expression to me of the untapped excellence that lies within us all. Not just as she played the piano but also as those same fingers brought music from a group of young hearts to ours. After visiting numerous places where discord and chaos rang in our ears, coming to this place has moved me deeply. Order and intonation have been restored to young lives. For days, until this moment, we have been

viewing people in the rough, illiterate and pitiable. Today, however, we are seeing those same people three or four years away from that old life—filled with truth and wholeness.

Father, I have been moved to reflect on those you have given us at home. People in the rough—illiterate (at least spiritually), thinking they have everything but having nothing that matters. Deaf and unable to hear the real music of life. Needing the same order I have seen here today. The harmony did not come easily. It took years. Paul said it should be "aimed at." To see all desiring to be one voice is heart-rending.

Lord, make me ever alert to Satan's desire for our people to go back to confusion, disharmony, and drum-beating. May I never forget this day, December 10, 1971.

Experiences such as the one in Jamaica taught me that nothing but our very best was good enough for Christ.

Some six years after coming to Collinsville, both Gordon and I sensed that we had reached a crossroads in our ministry among those wonderful people. It would be hard to describe all of the elements that make up an awareness that a special moment has come, but one knows when it is there. We realized that it was either time to dig in for a number of years into the future and adopt newer programs and policies or else turn the work over to somebody else who could perhaps take it in a slightly different direction. We wrestled with that decision for several months. The issue was, of course, complicated by our affection for the people who had poured so much into our lives.

Besides, our children were happy with their home and their congregation. For each member of my family, the thought of having to say goodbye was unbearable, and yet goodbye seemed inevitable.

Do you believe that a life submitted to God has no chance

occurrences? If you do, then you would have to ask the meaning of three men, unknown to one another, calling within a short time to say that they have recommended the name of Gordon MacDonald to a New England church seeking a pastor. It seemed uncanny to us that these men could have known that for the first time in years both Gordon and I were open to a possible change in our ministry!

The time to separate from our Southern Illinois congregation had come—that had become increasingly clear to both of us. Not because we'd come to love the people any less, but because we had quietly concluded that the next phase of their life as a church might best be led by someone else. We also sensed a growing hunger within our spirits to tackle new challenges, to enlarge the scope of our experience with various kinds of people, and perhaps to be in a place where we could extend our efforts at influencing and training young men and women for service in ministry.

That was the backdrop for the evening when a strange voice on the telephone identified itself as a representative of Grace Chapel, an interdenominational congregation in Lexington, Massachusetts. We later learned it was a beautiful suburban community saturated in American history outside of Boston.

Like many pastors, Gordon has received numerous invitations to consider opportunities when various churches are seeking pastoral leadership. Some have been churches much larger in size than either First Baptist of Collinsville or even Grace Chapel, for that matter. But it is interesting that neither Gordon nor I has ever been attracted to situations simply because they were larger or seemed more prestigious.

But there was something different about the query from Grace Chapel. A spiritual magnet was drawing us, it seemed, to Lexington by way of the voice on the phone and later through letters.

Is there a good way to leave a church? It was difficult to convince some of our people that a decision to conclude our

184

ministry in Southern Illinois had been made from a positive perspective. A few felt hurt that we could actually consider leaving them. Some even felt compelled to find negative reasons to explain why Gordon would ever want to leave. One or two were convinced that he wanted more money or even a larger congregation. Others became self-critical, convinced that they simply weren't good enough for us.

To the less-than-mature Christians, our explaining that a time of natural parting between the congregation and its pastor had come was very hard. However, the more spiritually perceptive and mature members of the congregation seemed to understand Gordon's decision and gave us their blessing.

The fact is that the ministry is fraught with a series of hellos and goodbyes. Unfortunately, in some cases, the goodbyes are said in the wake of a failure or a breakdown in rapport with a congregation. Thankfully, that was not the case during our time in Collinsville. The fact that we had a pleasant and ongoing relationship with our people did not make the separation any easier, however!

I've since come to understand what C. S. Lewis was saying when he wrote, "I loathe saying goodbyes." Now my family says, "We'll be seeing you." That last month in Collinsville, after we decided that it was time to leave, was one of the hardest of our lives. Everyone did his best to express thanksgiving and appreciation to our family, and we in turn kept trying to find ways to say that we loved them. A thousand tears were shed. We found ourselves eating in many homes for breakfast, lunch, and dinner. It was a delightful, but emotionally draining, time.

When the final goodbyes had been said and the last service had been held, it came time for us to leave. The moving van had come and gone. Our belongings were headed in an easterly direction—to New England, where the next phase of our lives would begin. As we drove out of that Southern Illinois community for the last time, I could sense that we were leaving behind a group of Christians who were at different places in their spiritual maturing process. We had watched some men and women grow to become utterly dependable in serving the Lord. Others were brand-new Christians, and it seemed as if their pilgrimage in faith had only begun. It was that latter group for whom I felt a stab of conscience. Were we abandoning them? Should we have stayed longer to oversee their growth toward maturity?

I was again comforted by the words of Helen Roseveare about the necessity of saying goodbyes. She reminded me that you cannot be the last link in everybody's chain of experience. Now I know that she's absolutely right! None of us can be the last link. For some in Collinsville, we had been the first link in giving them an opportunity to find Christ and begin a new life. For others we were the middle link, urging them on to maintain commitments made previously. And, to our delight, we were for a few others, in a sense, the last link helping them to accelerate into maturity and the joys of life grounded in Jesus Christ. It was a humbling, but nevertheless peaceful, experience to realize that we were simply links in a congregation's spiritual chain of growth. Others would come in behind us, continue the job, and then hand it on to still others.

Closing the Collinsville chapter of our lives was not easy —in a sense we've never closed it. To this day whenever a letter arrives from Southern Illinois, we open it eagerly, hoping to hear news about the people. We're happy as we read about the ones who are getting married or who are having their first children; these are people we knew as infants and toddlers in the Sunday school departments. Some have headed to the mission field or accepted positions of leadership within the Collinsville congregation. The memories of their receiving Christ as Savior and growing in the faith are still quite vivid to us.

What made our memories of Collinsville so precious? Our choice to love the people. They in turn had loved us and together we had all learned to love Christ a bit more.

3
Becoming Yankees

There was a day when I died, utterly died—died to George Müller, his opinions, preferences, tastes and will—died to the world, its approval or censure—died to the approval or blame even of my brethren or friends—and since then I have studied only to show myself approved unto God. George Müller

LOOKING back at the flow of events which led us from Illinois to Massachusetts, I recall the anxieties Gordon and I once shared when he was still a senior in seminary and could see our dreams hanging like wisps of the future.

"Will *anyone* ever be interested in our pastoral service?" we wondered, worrying ourselves into a frenzy of despair. "After all that education, will anyone really want us? Are we fit for the job? Is it that tough to get along with a congregation?" Questions like those almost consumed us for a while.

Today when I hear them from young, potential pastors and their spouses, I caution myself to be extra gentle. We were uneasy once too, but now having experienced a variety of congregations, I am quick to respond that God does indeed know our individual addresses and the areas in which we are best suited to serve him.

God knew what he was doing when he brought the people of Grace Chapel and the MacDonald family together —and the people of the other earlier congregations too! Our weekend visit to Lexington when the congregation had heard Gordon preach and answer endless questions had come and gone. By the time we'd flown out of Boston on Monday morning, we were already entranced by the possibilities at Grace Chapel. We hoped the people had liked us as much as we had liked them.

The weekend had been relatively pressure free, probably due to the fact that neither Gordon nor I had felt constrained to impress anyone. Of course we had wanted to be at our very best since people had been noting the type of persons we were, but we had tried to relax and to be as open as possible. A quiet inner confidence had come, I believe, from the Holy Spirit so that we could leave the results of the weekend to the Lord. Three days later those results were to become evident.

After getting an enthusiastic call, Gordon was quick to accept the invitation of the Grace Chapel family. The next day we immediately embarked upon the bittersweet experience of disengaging from one congregation which we greatly loved and of entering a new relationship with people we sensed God wanted us to be serving in the near future.

When you are happy where you are, a pastoral resignation is an almost unbearable experience. As I've said before, goodbyes are difficult. We had to leave people who remain our friends to this day. But we did have to say "so long" and made it quite clear that once we were gone, the people of First Baptist Church in Collinsville would have to look to another spiritual leader and give him the love and the loyalty that they had once given us. For some people, especially those for whom we had become spiritual parents, that was a very hard thing to do.

When we left Collinsville, we purposely reserved several weeks to ourselves in order to "drop out." Friends made a cottage by the shore of Lake Erie in Ohio available to us, and we used their generous gift as a place to read, to talk, to pray, and to enjoy a brief and rare privacy with our children. It was nice to be someplace where no one knew us or even cared about who we were. We could feel the hand of God upon our lives, filling us each day with new energy and expectation about the future.

Gordon and I immersed ourselves in the writings of Elton Trueblood, A. W. Tozer, Paul Tournier, Dietrich Bonhoeffer, and E. Stanley Jones. Each of them had much to give us, especially since our anticipation and excitement had become slowly tempered with an awareness that New England was not the easiest place in which to launch a pastoral ministry.

We'd begun to hear frightening stories about New England. Some called it the "graveyard of ministers." One famous preacher had written that New England churches were so cold that one could ice-skate down the center aisle on a Sunday morning. The coldness he referred to had nothing to do with the physical temperature. The liberal, secular attitudes in the public school system tempted us to worry about the influences our children would face when they entered school in the fall.

Had we made a mistake? Collinsville, after all, had been a comfortable place for our family. Would New England indeed be our graveyard, the place of failure for our family? Would we be accepted or would people look down upon our Midwestern acculturization?

After the respite on Lake Erie, we drove eastward with a mixture of hope and anxiety. More and more I found myself dwelling upon the need to become conformed to the image of Christ. I truly wanted to be a woman "adorned" with godliness. I wanted our new congregation to see me as a supportive wife, a faithful Christian, and a good mother. Most of all, I wanted the people at Grace Chapel to see Christ fleshed out in the roles of my existence.

During our vacation on Lake Erie, I had determined to

pursue a more energetic search for my priority spiritual gifts. After finding them, I would begin to pursue them in earnest. I had also resolved to enhance my spiritual disciplines by a more thorough use of my personal journal for recording insights and by a more systematic reading of Scripture and the great Christian thinkers. Finally, I'd determined to get better control of my time, carefully monitoring the flow of relationships around me so that I wouldn't be consumed to an unhealthy extent again.

Deep inside me was the drive to try to please everybody. I was a "doer," so how could I discipline myself and resist the trap of burning out? Sarah Edwards, the wife of Jonathan Edwards, had once struggled with the same problem. Her biographer Elizabeth Dodds writes, "One hurdle Sarah still had to surmount was her need to be liked by everyone."[1] Sarah and I could have had some good talks about a common weakness.

Gordon and I knew that we were entering a congregation that had deeply loved its former pastor. He had been there for ten years and had, along with his wife, served the people well. When they'd left, more than one person had asked whether the church could actually survive. Now, in our wistful moments, we were tempted to ask whether that former pastor's shoes could be filled. Would the church accept new leadership? Would we come out on the short end of constant comparisons?

This was a new state of affairs to us since in the previous two congregations the preceding pastor had left under duress and friction. It had thus been relatively easy for the people to respond to Gordon out of a desire to forget their past. Things were different now.

But love comes in unlimited amounts, I concluded. If the Grace Chapel congregation had loved its former pastor, it probably had enough love left over for us. Moreover, if we set out to pursue the same policy we had at Collinsville— loving people unconditionally and affirming their past and present—perhaps the new people would begin to respond to us and love us too.

By the time we passed the "Entering Lexington" sign which signaled the end of our long trip, the Lord had put our minds at ease and convinced us that he had everything under control. Our children would be safe as long as we maintained our family disciplines. New England would not become our "graveyard" provided we maintained our spiritual disciplines. And, yes, the congregation would accept us if we concentrated on being true to the biblical disciplines of ministry. As for myself? I need not turn out to be like the snapshot that Howard Hendricks once described as "overexposed and underdeveloped."

Charles H. MacKintosh understood something of our anxieties when he wrote:

> Happy the man who ministers (Christ), whatever be the success or reception of his ministry. For should the ministry fail to attract attention, to command influence, or to produce apparent results, he has his sweet retreat and his unfailing portion in Christ, of which nothing can deprive him. Whereas, the man who is merely feeding upon the fruit of his ministry, who delights in the gratification which it affords, or the attention and interest which it commands, is like a mere pipe, conveying water to others, and retaining only rust in itself. There is a most deplorable condition of every servant who is more occupied with his work and its results, than with the Master and His glory.[2]

God answered our prayers in several ways and gently addressed those fears which the typical pastor and his spouse bring into a new situation.

Take our concern about the children and their experience in public school. Two days after we were settled in our new home, the principal at Mark and Kristi's school invited them to visit the school and see their schoolrooms before classes began in a couple of weeks. Gordon looked at me in amazement. "Think of it!" he said, putting down the phone. "We thought this was going to be a depersonalized school system, and the principal calls and issues a personal invitation to come down to the school!"

The following day Gordon and the children visited the school and discovered that the principal was a Christian layman. He had been anxious to make our children's entrance into the new school as trouble-free as possible. That evening we literally wept as we realized that God had spoken directly to our fears about our children's education. They went on to have the finest public school experience we could possibly ask for. "See, I told you that I had everything under control," the Lord was saying in effect.

If New England was a cold region, especially in the churches, then we certainly didn't see it. Right away Grace Chapel began moving along with Gordon's style and his emphasis upon relationships and Christian character-building. Services were marked with silence and reverence, laughter and holy joy. Attendance at the various services began to increase almost immediately.

On one of the very first Sundays Gordon was greeted at the back of the sanctuary by a young man with a solemn face. The wrinkled clothes, shaggy beard, and long hair frightened Gordon a bit, he later confessed. So bracing himself, Gordon stuck out his hand and asked, "What can I do for you?"

"Did you mean what you said this morning?" the young man asked.

"What do you mean?" Gordon responded.

"About forgiveness . . . that we can come to God and find complete forgiveness and get right with him."

"Absolutely," Gordon said.

"Then that's exactly what I want. How do I get it?"

Gordon could hardly believe what this representative of

the counter-culture was saying. Thirty minutes later the two of them were kneeling and praying about forgiveness —Gordon in a three-piece suit and this young, jean-clad man named Tony.

A few weeks later Gordon married Tony and his girl friend, Chris. Today they are important members of the Grace Chapel family. We've watched them grow spiritually and begin to raise a beautiful family of their own.

The big challenge for me, as always, has been living out my role as pastor's wife in a ministry marked by balance and effectiveness. As I began to find my place in the congregation, I found Paul's admonition to Timothy:

> Work hard so God can say to you, "Well done" (2 Timothy 2:15, TLB)

coming up again and again. Each day I began by reminding myself that the *key issue is gaining the approval of God* for my actions and attitudes as wife, mother, and woman.

As you pursue the goal of God's approval, you begin to learn that there is a high cost to pay. Women who want to enjoy the privileges of leadership must simply face that fact. Leadership is never cheap. We mustn't deceive ourselves about how expensive it really is.

When David, king of Israel, wanted to establish a place of worship and sacrifice to God for the benefit of his people, he was offered a free plot of land. The Bible says that he refused to accept it as a gift because he knew that he couldn't offer the Lord something that had cost him nothing. Thus he made sure that the land was paid for properly.

Jesus highlighted the principle of costs when he pointed out the gifts of the widow at the temple offering box. He also made note of the boy who'd brought a small lunch to a large gathering and offered it for everyone to eat. Of one woman's gift he said:

> She has done a beautiful thing to me. (Mark 14:6)

In each case, Christ was not concerned about the exact value of the gift. What impressed him was what it had cost the person who gave it.

The privilege of having leadership in a church like Grace Chapel means counting the cost. Dale Evans Rogers writes:

> It is my conviction that when one chooses to live a public life in any profession, one should first count the cost of living such a life and not whimper at its pressures.[3]

I have had frequent conversations with women who never counted the cost before they faced the reality of ministry. Among those have been women whose husbands decided to enter the ministry after a number of years in the business world. For such women the rules of the game seemed to change abruptly, and they often followed their husbands unaware of the real cost of ministry. I have known some women who refuse to pay the cost and go through each day kicking and screaming. They pursue their own careers or they become increasingly embittered about a lifestyle that they never originally bargained for. Then again, I have known those who have struggled with the cost and have chosen to pay it. This is not to say that everything became tranquil for them—only that in that situation they began to grow. But when it comes to assessing the cost of leadership, I would never want to minimize the fact that pain is involved.

As the cost of ministry has become more plain to me in recent years, I have generally found myself ready and willing to pay it. I had been eager from the beginning to do what Gordon and I came to Lexington to accomplish. The choice having been made, I had set out to pursue the approval of God and the effectiveness of ministry insofar as I could contribute to it.

I quickly began to learn *the necessity of sharing my ministry with others.* Not sharing my ministry had been one of my original blindspots. I had failed to trust others adequately. Why? Because my standards had been so high that I'd felt compelled to do most things all by myself. And that was plainly wrong!

At Grace Chapel I came to realize that I too was surrounded by competent people. It was important that I free them to use their gifts and capabilities. Often I only had to step out of the way and let them perform.

Jethro, father-in-law to Moses, gave the leader of the Hebrews some advice that I also needed. The Bible says that Jethro was horrified by the weight Moses was carrying as leader to the people and stressed to Moses the importance of delegating and sharing ministry with others. Fortunately, Moses listened and quickly decentralized his leadership responsibility. It meant letting others accomplish agreed-upon goals in their own way and style, not necessarily as Moses himself would have done it. It was a great idea, and it worked for Moses. As I've employed it, it has also worked for me.

Sharing the load means ceasing to be a lone wolf and becoming a team person. We saw its delights and stresses first in the area of our pastoral staff. As Grace Chapel began to enjoy fast growth, we had to expand the pastoral staff with more men and women who could pick up the load. One of the heaviest responsibilities Gordon has had to bear is picking people to be part of that team. A wrong choice can be a disaster. Now my husband has a large number of pastors and specialists on his staff for whom he is responsible. This multiplication of staff relationships, including spouses and children, has meant that pastoring a staff alone is a full-time job.

Teamwork brings together people of differing work styles and spiritual values. If the team is to be unified and effective, and if the team relationship itself is to be a model of Christian love for the congregation, then the team has to be spiritually and administratively monitored and pastored.

That is a challenge that Gordon has learned to adjust to, but it hasn't been easy. The extra responsibility has often caused him to withdraw from maintaining contact with some of the congregation. But through all of the changes and the restructuring, Gordon has enjoyed amazing cooperation from the staff around him.

Both Gordon and I found as we grew in this experience that not every spouse of a staff member wished to be treated in the same way. Each spouse had come to the staff at a different level of spiritual maturity. All differed in their sense of how deeply they wished to be involved in the church. Some wanted to pursue an outside career; others needed to remain home with their children; and a few others wanted to be heavily involved with their husbands in the work of the congregation.

Because all of us lack complete insight into one another, I quickly learned that conflicts and misunderstandings could arise among us. Something said in a casual moment could be misinterpreted. An administrative decision which might be contrary to the desires of a staff pastor could easily alter the relationship between me and the wife of the man involved. It was hard for me to learn how to relate in Christian fellowship, knowing all the time that Gordon had to be involved in sound administration and accountability.

On a few occasions we found that a staff wife would attempt to bring something to my attention that her husband was hesitant to share with Gordon. I had to learn to keep out of business matters and force information and decisions back into the proper channels at the office.

Another thing we had to wrestle with was the matter of social relationships. Should the staff remain essentially aloof from the congregation when it came to pursuing close friendships in the church? Should the matter be left to individual discretion? Ultimately the staff chose the latter, but we have all seen examples of how the spiritual Enemy of the church can exploit friendships and jeopardize the vital unity of a staff.

Today at Grace Chapel, Gordon and I enjoy an unusually powerful team experience. The men and women around Gordon do everything they can to support him—and not simply because Gordon and his associate, Lyle Jacobson, have recruited and trained many of them. People in the congregation comment upon the quality of their friendship and their ability to carve out effective working relationships as co-leaders.

But if the staff enjoys effectiveness today, it is because all of us have worked so hard to iron out the wrinkles of misunderstanding and potential conflict. Both Gordon and I have tried never to allow friction to come between ourselves and other staff members. Wherever there has been a problem, Gordon has gone right to the heart of the matter. I've attempted the same as I've tried to cultivate supportive friendships with staff wives.

When asked to speak to young women whose husbands are headed towards staff ministries, I strongly urge them not to goad their husbands to become disloyal to the team or the team leader. I know something about the kind of support a person at the head of a pastoral staff desperately needs. It's easy for a young wife to tempt her husband to deny his pastoral boss the support the leader needs if he's going to give quality leadership. However, no one can learn to be a leader until he or she has first been a faithful follower.

Learning to share the load became a challenge even in my ministry with lay people. In teaching a weekly Bible study, I had to begin to train women to serve as core group leaders. Because of the incredible team of women who serve with me, God has given us both numerical and spiritual growth in our weekly Bible study.

At first I found myself tempted to force the women who worked with me to act and to move only in ways which suited *my* style. Is that dangerous tendency characteristic of organizations and movements led by women? Are women more prone than men to feel uneasy when things do not follow a rigid pattern of procedure? The end result is the squelching of both creativity and individual motivation.

As I adopted a policy of accepting diversity on the team, I saw women steadily mature. The free flow of ideas has enabled us all to become more effective. We have slowly learned that we need to maintain a balance between adherence to mutually agreed upon goals and the freedom to be ourselves, learning from one another.

During the past ten years Gordon and I have learned about *another cost of leadership: loneliness.* Leadership of any kind, not only in a church, has loneliness built into it. Many people have looked at Gordon and me and told us that our position seems most enviable. They see us at the center of wonderful people and assume that life with so many fine relationships must be a glamorous whirl. While it is true that we are quite happy, it is also just as true that loneliness is a reality in our experience.

A very trusted layman in our Illinois congregation once wrote to Gordon about this matter of loneliness:

> I am sure you have had your share of adversity as that is God's method of strengthening his servant. Thinking of the special kind of testing that befalls those servants of the Lord in high positions of leadership, I was reminded again of Elijah calling down fire from heaven to consume the offering so that "all may know that the Lord is God," and then within hours of that great event, he began to entertain thoughts that he was the only one left worshipping the Lord. What loneliness there must be in leadership such as yours. I would that I could make it less lonely, but know that it goes with the position. Hence my prayers. Know that my respect and love are with you to help alleviate the loneliness and the burden.

The writer of this insightful letter not only understands

the reality of loneliness, but also appreciates the danger inherent in it. His warning that our loneliness not be twisted into an "Elijah complex" is very helpful.

Where does loneliness come from? Well, partially from having to be responsible. How many times Gordon and I have sat up late into the evening, pondering the right decision or course of action concerning the congregation! I can think of times when strong-minded people, each seeming to have the mind of God, all differed, and Gordon would have to make a decision that would appear to affirm one opinion and repudiate the other.

Gordon and I have also known moments when someone we really trusted failed us, and it seemed impossible for us to find a graceful way to handle things. Loneliness can come during the process of pushing people toward higher spiritual standards when they find it more convenient to live at a lower level. And there is loneliness if you believe that God can be served more excellently and that staff and lay people can work harder to serve the King of Kings.

Loneliness has also come as the result of pursuing wisdom and insight. The older I get, the more I realize that we depend less on skill and more on wisdom when it comes to doing the work of Christ. Decision making, the use of confrontation or healing words, and accepting accountability for a large congregation and its diverse needs have all made Gordon and me turn inward to hear the still, small voice of God for direction and guidance. It becomes increasingly clear to me why wise people do not covet higher positions or greater responsibility unless God has anointed them for it. They are already aware of the loneliness of being the only ones to make an ultimate decision or to assume responsibility.

Gordon and I have often smiled about the fact that he faces few simple decisions. No leader ever gets the easy ones. The obvious decisions are always made by someone before they reach the desk of the senior pastor. They're made by people who can skillfully take policy and precedence and produce solutions. The decisions that Gordon has to make are the ones without precedent and probably without a totally right answer. In such situations he can often use me as a sounding board if I'm willing to listen. He can also find in me a prayer partner so that both of us can draw upon the promised wisdom of God.

A newly initiated pastor's wife wrote to me:

> There is no clear way to express the pastoral weight to those outside of it . . . it defies communication except to kindred spirits.

The experience of loneliness is heightened sometimes by an unfortunate attitude on the part of certain people in any congregation or movement. I'm thinking of those who have one of two dangerous attitudes: *that of desiring to see a leader fail* or *that of putting a leader on a pedestal as the essence of perfection*.

I suspect that the first attitude springs from the view that if a leader fails, there will be a lessening of the spiritual standards that the followers have to pursue. Occasionally I've seen a leader goaded by a person hoping to prod anger or vindictiveness. Is the idea one of trying to bring a leader down to a level where he or she can be handled?

On one occasion I heard a person accuse my husband of not giving firm enough leadership to a situation in the church. He was admonished to be tough and to stamp out any opposition to his goal. Minutes later, he was told by a second person in the church that he had no business assuming so much authority in that same matter and that he was not to think that he was running the church! If Gordon had been in a fighting mood or had had a difficult time maintaining self-control, that could have been a bad moment.

Under pressures like that, a pastor and his wife will benefit from listening carefully, learning what is truthful, and then retreating into quietness so that they can lay it all before the Lord. Only then should a response be formulated. A good wife can help her husband do that sort of thing. She can sense when he's near the breaking point, and she can make sure that he regains his perspective before any damage is done.

The second danger comes from the person who constantly makes a superstar out of a pastor or a leader. Could it be that people sometimes do that so that they can dismiss themselves from having to pursue the higher spiritual standard that a leader is setting? (Don't both dangers have that similar effect?) How terribly vulnerable a pastor and his wife are when people think that they can do no wrong, that they can never fail, that they can withstand any shock.

I like to warn pastors' wives to be aware of their husbands becoming the targets of too much praise, for then they are on dangerous footing. Since the temptation to believe totally the things that people say is a strong one, one needs to discriminate between honest affirmation and insipid flattery. The former is desperately needed; the latter is definitely destructive.

Loneliness is indeed part of the cost of leadership, but no one in our family resents it. We've faced the problem by developing a close marital relationship, a strong sense of family intimacy with our children, and a few intense friendships with our staff and with others facing similar challenges in Christian service.

We've found that developing close, personal friendships *within* the congregation has its drawbacks. As much as we'd love to nurture that kind of friendly relationship, we've had to draw back a bit. Why? Simply because we've discovered the great potential such friendship has for misunderstanding, hurt feelings, and the breaking of confidences.

When the day comes that a person needs the ministry of his pastor yet hasn't known him as anything but a "buddy," then what? To whom can the person turn for comfort or guidance? If the person needs to hear a word of rebuke or admonishment, a "buddy" pastor will be hard put to give it to him.

Because of the potential for hurt feelings, the smaller the congregation, the more difficult it is to have close relationships with members of the congregation. In a larger church, however, members have greater opportunities for friendships among themselves. As a result, whom the pastor's family becomes close to seems less important and less obvious. A larger church will also generally have one or more assistant pastors who can share the responsibilities of caring for the "flock."

We've become freer to maintain stronger ties with the parents of our children's friends because we believe such contact is natural and vital for the sake of our children. Obviously, the confidentiality issue is present in any size congregation. Hopefully, by the time we might pastor a larger congregation, however, we shall have more nearly mastered the disciplines of the controlled tongue!

One of the biggest drawbacks to developing very close friendships with members of a congregation is that the pastor's wife may find herself caught in the middle of an unpleasant tangle. Recently I spoke with a woman who has been very close to her pastor's wife. Another woman in the fellowship has reacted negatively to that relationship —to the point of making direct, verbal attacks on the pastor's wife. The situation has become a mass of misunderstood motives and hurts involving other people as well. No one seems able to unravel the knot of discord which immaturity and a spirit of envy have helped fashion.

While a measure of loneliness is inherent in leadership, loneliness may be a type of mixed blessing as it might preclude discord within the body of the congregation. Certainly, that insight holds true especially within the small church, as I've suggested earlier.

As we became Yankees in New England, the Lord began

to teach us more and more about what I call the *shepherd's instinct*. A shepherd knows when his flock needs to be led to better feeding grounds, when the sheep must be protected from danger, and when it is time for changes to be made.

When it comes to "feeding grounds," we've learned the importance of sensing the moods of Christian people for whom we are spiritually responsible. Gordon's journals have shown that our congregations have periods of emotional fluctuation just as individuals do. If a leader can sense moments of stress or opportunity before anyone else, he can help prepare people for what they are going to face.

We noted that February and March are particularly stressful months in New England. During the winter the temperatures here are very cold, and people have to work harder to keep themselves going in the routine. Harsh weather makes cars undependable; getting to work becomes a daily challenge. Older people are often on edge due to the risk of falling on ice and to the problems engendered by snow shoveling and by their bodies being vulnerable to the colder temperatures. All of that raises everyone's stress level.

According to his biographer, Jonathan Edwards also "slumped in March." Because even the best of us find times like these to be an uphill battle, it's important that spiritual leaders adjust their expectations. We must expect people's performances to be substandard occasionally. Then again we may be able to prepare them ahead of time so that there will be a marginal number of defeats. That's the job of the person with a shepherd's instinct.

Shepherds also have to *lead people through experiences of change*—especially those which are challenging or painful. All things, except God, are in a state of change. We change even though some of the changes are not to our liking. Churches also change, and that often makes people uncomfortable.

Doesn't a growing church delight everyone? No! Growth

means change, which means new faces, new programs, and new leadership. All of us like to talk about our desire to see a church grow, but not all of us are really ready to face the implications of change. More than one young pastor has resigned from a church because he had become a success in attracting people, but a failure in shepherding them to cope with the continuing changes of a growing congregation.

Gordon and I have tried to share with our people at Grace Chapel that change through growth has been painful for us too. I suspect that many feel that we naturally rejoice in the large numbers of people coming through the doors. To some extent we have, since it means that the world around us is being reached in a small way. But Gordon and I have also faced the frustration of trying to know people and be close to those who would like to be better acquainted with us. Because of the limits on our time and our capacity, we have often gone away from the church with the feeling that we let somebody down. And there is little joy in that.

I think the ultimate change for any of us comes when we realize that the time has come to step aside and let a young person assume the work that we have begun. Since I've been in Lexington, I've become more aware that I'll someday have to step down and that the time to prepare for it is right now. Thus, we need to be grooming our successors to take over the work that we've begun. We need to prepare people to accept a new leader, and finally, we ourselves need to be ready for the pain created as we pass along an opportunity or a responsibility.

In his book, *While It Is Day,* Elton Trueblood writes of an English educator who assumed the principalship of a school when he was forty-five. On the first day at his desk he wrote himself a letter to be opened at the age of sixty-five. In it he admonished himself to remember that everyone was replaceable and that there were numerous forty-five-year-old people who were ready and anxious to take the place of a man of sixty-five. Interestingly enough, Elton Trueblood writes, when the principal reached sixty-five, he became increasingly reluctant to make the changes necessary for a successor to take over. However, when he read his own letter written twenty years before, he was able to appropriate its message and began to pave the way for someone else.

E. Stanley Jones challenges me in the same way. He warns of what he calls, "limelight-itis," a spiritual sickness which grows on us when we need the applause of people rather than the approval of God. Facing a serious stroke which denied him opportunity to continue his ministry, he was undaunted. "Surrender to Jesus was the primary thing,"[4] he wrote. Jones was not bound by the need to keep sole grip on his responsibilities. There were others, he reasoned, who could take over and do just as well.

The challenge is to know how to master change at every level in our lives. Preparation for it is an ongoing experience; when a woman chooses to bind herself to an unchanging God, then she too can live with considerable freedom in a swiftly changing world. She can face change and she can also create it.

During my years with Gordon at Grace Chapel, I've learned that the shepherding instinct also includes *the development of a calming influence among people.* When the sheep are frightened by something mysterious, then the shepherd has to move among them, restoring their sense of stability and serenity. A pastor and his wife can do that if they are prepared.

Recently Gordon and I sat in a gymnasium and watched our son, Mark, play in a high school basketball game. The coach of the opposing team suddenly lost his temper with the referee, and the team was charged with a technical foul. We soon saw his team absorb the anxiety from the bench. Before long the captain of the team had another technical foul. Slowly his team disintegrated and they ended up losing the game badly. As we left the gym, Gordon and I commented on the graphic illustration of how a leader's mood can poison the demeanor of an entire group.

Conversely, I am impressed as I read of the time when Jesus stood among a crowd of Pharisees who had brought him an adulterous woman. The prevailing mood was hostile and revengeful, but Christ remained above the mood and slowed everything down by his silence. Stooping to write in the sand and remaining in total control of himself, he broke the momentum of the moment. When he was finished, the confrontation was diffused by a simple statement, and the woman was restored rather than destroyed.

Jesus acted in a similar way in the Garden of Gethsemane when faced with his captors. While they were frenzied, his demeanor was calm and forthright. Even Peter forgot everything he'd been taught as he lashed out with his sword. Peter could serve as a negative model of the way many of us often act under relational stress. How important it is that a leader learn to develop a cool and determined manner in the midst of crisis! Those of us in various kinds of pastoral leadership must acquire this discipline. One or two calm persons in a crowd of frightened people can usually restore confidence and stability.

That principle faced me one morning when I answered the telephone and found out that my younger brother was dying. As I heard the news, I was aware that my children, my friends, and the congregation would be watching me closely to see my reaction. The picture of our Lord's response to Lazarus' death came to me, and I determined to learn from Jesus that even death must not cause us to panic or to rush needlessly.

Gordon and I had already found out in Kristi's turpentine emergency that God was present in the midst of our trouble. Some days after that phone call, Gordon presided at my brother Jim's funeral. I saw how important it was that Gordon and I, even in the midst of our own grief, maintain strong right arms on which others could lean. We knew that God himself would give us the grace to help hurting sheep.

Our desire to serve people in the midst of frightening

moments has not come cheaply. It is in part the product of the anguish of our own lives. Both my husband and I have tasted the hurt of divorce, death, and tragedy in our immediate families. We know firsthand what happens when people get crushed or make mistakes for which no one seems to grant forgiveness. We are deeply sensitive to the single-parent, to the homosexual, to the mothers and the fathers who have given their very best only to feel total failure. Each time God has permitted Gordon and me to face family pressures like those, we have asked, "What can we learn from all of this?"

From our sensitivity has emerged a concern to minister to singles, to formerly married people, and to those who writhe in failure. Thus at Grace Chapel Gordon has tried hard to launch departments of ministry that would speak to the broken people of our world. The congregation has responded well, and we're delighted to see what is happening. But many of the good things that we now enjoy began from painful moments that we resolved never to let defeat us.

When the Apostle Paul was on his way to Rome, his ship was caught in a relentless storm. It appeared as if everyone would be lost at sea. Paul's composure in the midst of that crisis was marvelous! He emerged on deck and brought the people a word from the Lord.

Calm and order were restored, and everyone ultimately made it to shore. Others may have had the skill of a mariner, but it was Paul who had the sanity and the serenity that belong to a godly man. A performance like that comes only when someone has mastered the shepherd's instinct.

In a pastoral home, we are constantly aware of some tragedy: death, marital struggle, financial disaster, spiritual despair. We usually hear more bad news than good. Moments of fatigue leave one prey to the temptation of falling into self-pity: "How can we possibly bear up under all of this?" Let the self-pity grow for a while, and anyone in leadership will soon be rendered sterile, feeling exploited or even stepped on by everyone who seeks a scapegoat.

But that kind of thinking is simply diabolical. The fact is that God is trusting us with the privilege of sharing the most intimate moments of people's lives. We are being reached out to; people are trusting us when they are most vulnerable. They seek calmness and grace which they apparently cannot find anywhere else. A pastor and his wife must not resent a privilege like that.

We have numerous birch trees at Peace Ledge in New Hampshire. I'm always impressed with their resiliency. One winter when we had a lot of snow, a storm changed to sleet and coated the branches with so much ice that they finally bent all the way to the ground. They became frozen in that position. Then another layer of ice trapped them. All of the birches stayed that way for a couple of months. "Will they survive? Will they ever stand tall again?" we wondered.

They did! In the spring when the birches were standing tall again, I wrote in my journal:

> What a beautiful lesson the harsh winter and the resi-
> lient birches have given us. The birches can experience
> hardship, accept it, bend, but not break. They are flex-
> ible, not brittle. When relief comes, they are able to
> bounce back and experience the warmth and growth
> of spring. To resist is to break. O God, make me like a
> birch.

Susanna Spurgeon, the wife of the great English preacher became an invalid at thirty-three. She was thus always at home when her husband returned from the great tabernacle where thousands had come to hear him preach. Invariably he would be exhausted and depressed, partially the result of a condition which plagued him. As Charles Haddon Spurgeon attempted to recover from his sense of emotional emptiness, his wife would often read to him from Richard Baxter's book, *The Reformed Pastor*.

"He would weep," she said, "and I would weep too."[5] She was always sensitive and receptive to Charles' pain because she knew suffering in her own life. Watching an oak log burning in her fireplace, she observed, "We are like this old log; we should give forth no melodious sounds were it not for the fire."[6]

It seems that a certain amount of pain accompanys greatness, but if we give the pain to God, it can also become redemptive. Amy Carmichael's poem has moved me deeply:

> Before the winds that blow do cease,
> teach me to dwell within Thy calm;
> Before the pain has passed in peace,
> give me, my God, to sing a song.
> Let me not lose the chance to prove
> the fullness of enabling love,
> O love of God, do this for me;
> maintain a constant victory.[7]

I've also been moved by Thorton Wilder's play which deals with healing at the pool of Bethesda. A doctor, suffering from an incurable disease, draws near to the pool, hoping for a chance to enter it and find healing. However, before he can reach the edge, an angel restrains him:

> Draw back, physician. Healing is not for thee. Without your wounds, where would your power be? It is your sorrow that puts kindness in your face and makes your voice low so that it trembles in the hearts of men. The angels themselves cannot heal the wretched as can one human being broken on the wheel of life. In love's service, only the wounded can serve.[8]

During the time that we have been "Yankees," Gordon and I have learned another thing about the shepherding instinct: *In accepting the role of a model for others, the leader risks the loss of some privacy.*

In leadership, our personal lives and our marital relationships serve as models. To an extent our families also become models. Gordon and I know that people will look to see how we treat our children and how, in turn, our children respond to us.

When we came to Grace Chapel, our children were still quite young. During Sunday morning worship services, they sat with Gordon and me on the front row. Gordon would leave the family only when it was time for him to preach or to lead various portions of the service. One reason we sat together was simply to let the congregation see us as a family serving them and worshiping the Lord—just as we expected them to do.

There were various by-products of that discipline! The children loved getting as close to their Dad as they could. People could see his obvious affection for Mark and Kristi, and that, I believe, authenticated his ministry to everyone. For others, it was a modeling experience.

I am moved as I realize over and over again that some people have gained strength for their own relationships by watching Gordon and me relate together. One young man, a seminarian, shared with us that he and his fianceé, had deliberately sat behind our seats at Grace Chapel for many months. The young lady he wished to marry had been deeply hurt by the breakup of the marriage of her pastor years ago; she found it impossible to believe that a marriage in the pastoral ministry could actually be a healthy one. Her fiancé realizing that she needed to believe in that possibility again, encouraged her to be part of the congregation at Grace Chapel and watch Gordon and me. After several months of seeing us worshiping together, her heart was settled. Today that lovely couple serve Christ as pastor and wife in a Midwestern congregation.

Today our children are teenagers and sit more often with their friends. But as recently as last Sunday while I sat in the soprano section of the choir, I suddenly realized that our entire family was involved in some part of the worship service! Gordon was going to preach, of course, and there was Mark up in the balcony, serving as team leader for a group of ushers who man the balcony for our first service in the morning. Kristi was playing in the handbell group that was accompanying the choir on the anthem. I'm convinced that the joy of our family serving as a model today began with those early years of our being together on the front row, setting an example for other families in the church to follow.

We pursued the concept of teaching-by-modeling one year when we entertained eight seminary couples for six different nights in ways we thought would be useful for their future ministry. On one of those evenings in the midst of dinner, the doorbell rang and we were all confronted with a hysterical young woman who had a serious problem. The couples had a chance to watch us handle the scene, to see whether we could flex with the occasion. While Gordon continued to entertain the seminarians, I took the unexpected visitor to another room, where she and I were able to discuss the problem she was facing.

If a leader resents the loss of privacy and the fact that someone is always watching, the pastoral life can quickly become quite miserable. Yet which one of us doesn't yearn for some obscurity? Isn't there some irritation in knowing that you must always be at least reasonably attired should an unexpected caller come to the door? And isn't it tempting to think about how nice it might be to go to church one Sunday and not have a single conversation centered on a problem or a decision?

Whenever I'm tempted to think such self-pitying thoughts, I try to recall an unforgettable visit my husband and I made to the home of a missionary couple along the Ivory Coast in West Africa. The missionaries lived in a Muslim community and had no Christian fellowship for weeks at a time. Privacy was nonexistent in their village culture. Everyone felt free to enter anyone's home at any time during the day and sit watching what was going on for as long as he or she chose.

It was a price our missionary friends gladly paid because they loved the Muslim people. Instead of having privacy, they had allowed their home to become a sort of fishbowl so that people could see Christ in the routine of life. They had no regrets about their choice. And I have none about the choice that we've made in Lexington to give the marvelous people of our Yankee congregation a chance to see how Christ helps my family to grow and mature.

Nine years have come and gone. For us, New England is decidedly not a graveyard, but the birthplace for a vision. As in Sainty and in Collinsville, we have given much and have received much more in return. It would be hard for us to conceive of anything more exciting and fulfilling than our experiences among the people of our New England congregation. Somewhere along the way, we lost the tendency to worry about tomorrow. Today is more than enough to keep us challenged and satisfied.

My tale of three congregations is terribly incomplete. A thousand more stories could have been told, but time and space do not permit. The conclusion is really simple: When a man or a woman has heard God's call, when people are ready to march under sturdy and consistent spiritual leadership, when there is a desire to be all that God wants, then you will find the story of a congregation that is every bit as exciting as anything I've attempted to relate. The key will always be men and women in ministry who are unswervingly obedient to the Lord and sensitive to words such as those which Peter gave to spiritual leaders:

> *Tend the flock of God that is your charge, not by constraint but willingly, not for shameful gain but eagerly, not as domineering over those in your charge but being examples to the flock. And when the chief Shepherd is manifested you will obtain the unfading crown of glory.* (1 Peter 5:2-4)

4
We Are Wealthy People

I thank my God in all my remembrance of you, always in every prayer of mine for you all making my prayer with joy, thankful for your partnership in the gospel from the first day until now. (Philippians 1:3-5)

WHILE the calendar says it has been exactly twenty years, it actually seems only a few days ago that I heard Gordon give his first sermon, challenging a group of high school young people. He was attempting to share his discoveries in the Word of God. I clearly remember sitting in the audience with a mixture of pride and prayerful concern for his effectiveness.

Now two decades later those original feelings of excitement remain. The simple truth is that Gordon and I have never stopped loving the ministry. When there have been painful moments, they have always ultimately given way to joy and growth. We've had a long enough stretch of time to realize that everything that we've experienced has been worth it. There is no greater privilege for us than to serve people and watch them mature in Christlikeness!

For me the unequaled fulfillment has been in watching my husband's first love deepen, partially because we have been together. There is nothing he would rather do than preach. Samuel Chadwick, the great Methodist preacher of England, expressed it as, I believe, Gordon sees it:

> I have loved my job with a passionate and consuming love. I would rather preach than do anything else I know in this world. I've never missed a chance to preach. I would rather preach than eat my dinner, or have a holiday, or anything else the world can offer. I would rather pay to preach than be paid not to preach. It has its price in agony of sweat and tears, and no calling has such joys and heartbreaks, but it is a calling an archangel might covet; and I thank God that of his grace he called me into this ministry. Is there any joy like that of saving a soul from death? Any thrill like that of opening blind eyes? Any reward like the love of little children, to the second and third generation? Any treasure like the grateful love of hearts healed and comforted? I tell you, it is a glorious privilege to share the travail and the wine of God. . . . I wish I had been a better minister, but there is nothing in God's world or worlds I would rather be.[1]

I have learned again and again that this business of serving people is never a one-way street. The more we have loved people, the more we have been loved. The more we have served, the more we have been served. From a spiritual perspective, we have never gone "broke" as a result of our investments. While Gordon could have earned more money in another career, he and I have never thought of wealth in terms of a bank account. The fact is *we are very wealthy*.

Some people have their wealth in investments, safety deposit boxes, and in jewelry. Our wealth is found in far different places. *We've stored our wealth in the memory bank of our minds where we reall what people have done for us during moments of extreme need.*

I'm thinking of a Sunday when I felt, as some put it, "in the pits." If I had not been the wife of a pastor, I would have stayed home and probably enjoyed a bath in self-pity. I was very tired, weighted down by a series of circumstances which had fallen in on me all at the same time. But because it was part of my commitment to a congregation, I dutifully took my seat in the choir, hoping that something might fill up the empty spirit and numb feelings which I had taken to church with me.

My ears suddenly caught a familiar melody being played softly and sensitively by Bill Reed, our organist at Grace Chapel. He had obviously departed from playing his planned classical prelude. For some reason not obvious to me, he was playing a simple, well-known hymn instead. I knew the words by heart and allowed them to settle in on my exhausted spirit:

> Some through the waters, some through the flood,
> some through the fire, but all through the blood,
> God leads his dear children along. . . .

The words of that old hymn and the way it was played began to lift the cloud that had covered me. I soon found myself thanking the Lord that I had been ministered to in a very special way by the seemingly random choice our organist had made in changing his music for that day.

At the conclusion of the service Bill Reed met me in the choir room. Waiting until I was alone, he commented on the fact that I was not my usual "bubbly self." He'd read the expression on my face, he said, so he had immediately put his planned, practiced organ piece aside, and picked a song that he thought might reach out to me. *And that's exactly what had happened.* He had reached, and I had grabbed. I don't know when I have been so touched by the sensitivity of a Christian person who used his gift to minister to one he believed to be hurting. There is inestimable wealth when you have friends who care enough to notice when you are under pressure and then do something about it.

My memory bank also keeps recollection of *answered prayers*. For several years a childless couple had hoped that they could start a family. Time had passed and their hopes for a child seemed to be slipping away. The wife and I agreed to pray for a breakthrough in the problem. We asked others to join us, and God responded to our prayers. When a little girl was born, the couple made Gail the middle name of God's gift to them. Every time I see that little girl, I'm reminded of the intimate part God allowed us to share in that family's experience.

There are the memories of moments when Gordon and I have been invited into the intimate circle of a family that was suffering. I have been able to help a woman die with dignity and faith, and I have had the opportunity to listen as one or another has poured out insights and observations learned only in the most anguished moments of human existence. The privilege of being present on an occasion like that is invaluable. What amount of money could pay for the honor of being trusted?

Gordon and I are also wealthy in *spiritual trophies*. Try to assign a dollar value to the joy you feel when you see a couple whom you were able to help in overcoming tensions and struggles of whether or not to get married. Tell me how much you think it is worth to have the joy of seeing a pastor's wife whom you discipled in her teen years. Now she's a supportive helpmate and the mother of three PK's. What is it worth to have the pleasure of seeing a wife who has become a Christian and learned from you how to be patient with her husband so that she might wisely introduce him to Christ?

When the Grace Chapel family meets on Sunday, Gordon and I look across the sanctuary and see two couples sitting together. Five years ago one of those couples was on the verge of separation until the husband gave his life over to the lordship of Christ. The marriage was healed as a result. Now, several years later, we see a mature husband and wife sitting with another couple whose problems are similar to the ones that they had faced a few years ago. This time Gordon does not have to do any of the counseling or spiritual directing. The man he led to Christ five years ago can do it. Gordon and I only have to pray and watch with joy.

Some of our holdings of wealth are found in the *friendships* which we have with *people whose lives have been marked with incredible godliness.* We have always had in our congregations one or two very old men whose faith and stability have been a light to us. These unshakable men have lavished their encouragement, wisdom, and loyalty upon us. They have loved us with a quality of affection which only the aged comprehend. Both Gordon and I have grown because of such love.

Reinhold Niebuhr writes of a woman in his congregation who ministered in the same way to him:

> The way Mrs. —— bears her pains and awaits her ultimate and certain dissolution with childlike faith and inner serenity is an achievement which philosophers might well envy. I declare that there is a quality in the lives of unschooled people, if they have made good use of the school of life and pain, which wins my admiration much more than anything you can find in effete circles.
>
> Mrs. —— has had a hard life, raised a large family under great difficulties, is revered by her children, respected by her friends, and she has learned to view the difficult future with quiet courage as she surveys the painful and yet happy past with sincere gratitude. She thanks me for praying with her and imagines that I am doing her a favor to come and see her. But I really come for selfish reasons—*because I leave that home with a more radiant faith of my own.* My confidence in both man and God is strengthened.[2] (italics mine)

Our wealth is also in *people who serve us*. Both of our children have enjoyed friendships with older single adults. Norman, in his mid-twenties, has been a close personal friend to our son during his teen years. Through that friendship Mark has grown spiritually and has taken on traits which have been a delight to us. When I peek into his bedroom late at night and see him having his quiet time before he goes to sleep, I am aware that it is in part because he and Norman hold each other accountable for their walk with God.

Our daughter, Kristi, has been deeply influenced by a young college student named Vicki, whose faith and style of life have always been magnetic and attractive. Their many conversations have accrued in our daughter's spiritual maturity. Both Norman and Vicki have truly served our family!

Gordon has had the privilege of sharing ten years of ministry with our associate pastor, Lyle Jacobson. What a beautiful picture their relationship has been to the Grace Chapel family. Their lighthearted fun, their warm friendship, the absence of jealousy, and the special ways that they support one another have enhanced all of our lives. Many of the things which Gordon has accomplished in his life and ministry would never have been possible without Lyle's support.

I think of the women who've surrounded me with various spiritual gifts. One woman has taught me more by her sensitive giving than I could have ever learned from a hundred books. If I ask her for a recipe, as I've often done, she will more than likely drop off a copy of it a few days later along with all of the ingredients in the recipe. "It's a bit expensive to fix," she'll say, "so I thought I'd give you a good start." If she learns that I'll be entertaining for several nights in a row, she'll insist upon making a dessert or two for me or providing an appropriate centerpiece to take the pressure off me as I plan.

I have another friend in our congregation who makes it

her ministry to pray for me, to be my strong right arm of encouragement. In her gentle way, she'll regularly call me to find out how I am and what matters may need special intercession. Throughout the years she has faithfully ministered to me and never asked for a thing in return.

I am wealthy in the number of other women friends who support me administratively in my teaching of the Bible. They're committed to relieving me of all concerns except that of preparing for Bible teaching and helping the women of the Bible class to grow. I am amazed at the faithfulness of my helpers! Nothing is too small or menial for them to tackle if they know that it will help me.

There are those in our congregation who have learned to look for the earliest signs of fatigue in either Gordon or me. Upon seeing it, they have been quick to speak to us about it, urging us to get rest and spiritual fortification. We've been surrounded by elders and spiritual leaders in our congregation who have been only too willing to "lay hands" on Gordon when they knew that he was under enormous pressure to present important messages from the Grace Chapel pulpit. These have been the same people who have always been there to give Gordon their blessing and to pray for him when he has left to minister in some other part of the world.

My family and I also possess wealth through our *exposure to the fascinating lifestyles of the people we've served* in our three congregations. We have been the supper guests of a naval commander aboard a nuclear submarine. Gordon has walked (perhaps straddled) the steel beams of a tall building under construction as he has spent time with the foreman of a steel workers' crew. We have walked rounds with a physician, hammered nails with a carpenter, played games with a computer and its programmer, and befriended a professional football player.

We have witnessed the collapse of impressive and wealthy people. Conversely, we have seen the greatness of simple and poor people. We have laughed with people, cried with them, worried with them, and rejoiced with them. Every experience has added to our wealth.

If a farmer's economic holdings are to be found in the soil, our wealth has been found in our congregations where we have seen people grow. We have been around Grace Chapel just long enough now to see the fruition of a number of our theories and practices of ministry. We are seeing people who were teenagers just a few years ago now enter into careers and marriage as young adults. Having had the privilege of participating in their preparation, we like what we see. We have watched the growth of new Christians, who are now assuming congregational leadership. Having done some of the discipling that has brought them to maturity, we are pleased with the results. We are also observing young pastoral staff members at Grace Chapel who once started out as seminary interns. Having had a chance to make some contributions to their life and growth, we are thrilled with the way they speak and lead in wisdom and spiritual authority.

You would have to say that a *part of our wealth is also in what we see ourselves becoming.* The years have sharpened certain instincts within us. I am quietly amused when I sense that a person is troubled, tell her so, and find that she is shocked that I seem to know her so well. "How could you have ever guessed?" is the response. I really don't have much of an answer except that over the years the Holy Spirit has given me some insight into spotting broken and hurting people. I value that gift of insight. It was not acquired in a schoolroom but purchased through years of ministry.

Our wealth is also in the *lessons we've accumulated from God's Word, from extensive reading, and from things learned at the feet of great men and women of God* who have taught us by their example. We've experienced great joy in taking things learned in the midst of quiet study and then sharing them with spiritually hungry people.

Into our home have come people whom God has richly blessed. They have shown attention to our children, and my family has had the chance to see how Christ relates to our visitors. We have also enjoyed visiting missionaries, national pastors, leaders in other countries, and people newly open to the gospel of Christ. We are rich in the long chain of opportunities to serve which special people have made available to my husband and me.

Finally, perhaps the greatest wealth has come from *learning that God will never let a person down.* We have had a life of ministry too long now not to have seen God work in extraordinary ways. We realize that it is pointless to worry, to panic, to ever wonder what lies ahead, or to be concerned about someone else being better or getting more credit. More and more we've learned to let all of that rest in God's hands; little by little we have learned the lesson that it *must* be that way. We do not feel pressured to be part of a super large congregation. We don't have to know well-known people; our material possessions do not have to be the best or the newest. I believe that *one is truly wealthy when one is free from those spirit-withering pursuits.*

Who knows what lies ahead for Gordon and me? We are firmly locked into the middle years of life and even find ourselves wondering about retirement somewhere down the line. I am quite sure that there are still times ahead when one or both of us will want to quit in discouragement. And perhaps there will be other days when we think things are going so well that nothing could ever go wrong. But no matter how many more years there are, and no matter what direction we move in, I pray that we will grow to be more like Christ and be able to serve some portion of his great Church.

I have enormous respect for any woman who enters leadership or who chooses to marry a man who will be in leadership. I am well acquainted with the pressures and the possibilities she can experience. I hope she looks at them all with the same joy that I have been able to find in my own life. No matter where we find ourselves, there is work to do and there are opportunities to seize.

Whenever I reevaluate my commitment to the pastoral life to which God has called Gordon and me, I am reminded of the words of Hudson Taylor. At the age of sixty-two he wrote:

> God chose me because I was weak enough. God does not do his great works by large committees. He trains somebody to be quiet enough, and little enough, and then uses him.[3]

God was able to use Hudson, for he possessed the right kind of attitude. And alongside was Maria, a woman of whom it has been said:

> Undoubtedly the overriding factor in (the Taylor) marriage was an equal, uninhibited loyalty to their vocation. But without Maria, Taylor never could have embarked on his life's work.[4]

As long as God permits, I will pursue the goals of servant-shepherd, wife-confidante, and mother-supporter. For me, there can be no greater privilege and no higher calling.

APPENDIX
On the Gift of Hospitality

I'VE been amazed by the number of questions and comments about hospitality which come up time and time again in my discussions with women. Several have realized that the "open home" can be one of the most valuable aspects of ministry, but none have felt really confident about their knowledge of how to make their homes useful in this way. Here are several approaches to hospitality which I've found effective in making our home an inviting place to be.

In the past, we've been partial to *fondue parties,* as you've probably noticed earlier in the book. When we invite people from our carefully groomed guest list, we ask them to bring one pound of sirloin meat, cut into one-inch cubes. I've found it necessary to give *precise* instructions about the meat. Asking guests to bring their own meat helps cut down the cost of entertaining and makes it possible for you to entertain more frequently, so no need to feel skittish about it!

When the guests arrive on a fondue evening, we take their meat in exchange for a bag with five pieces of a puzzle. Each bag is labeled with the name of a group—Opera Singers, Jackhammers, Fire Trucks, etcetera. You can make up your own.

The guests are directed to our recreation room where they are instructed not to speak until they've identified their particular team. How do they discover their team members? By sounding like the object or person which represents their team name. You can imagine the hysterical laughter emanating from the rec room as people go around sounding like fire trucks, opera singers, and the like!

Give the guests time to find their "team mates." Then each team sorts out the puzzle pieces as a group. The first team to finish the puzzle wins the "prize" of being the first to partake of the salad and meat.

Why all of this? We've discovered that laughter and silliness break down barriers and seeming differences. They lend a lighthearted mood to the evening. The team effort in doing the puzzle also creates a sense of comraderie. In fact, people forget they're visiting the pastor's home!

Later during the mealtime, this cooperative attitude can be enhanced as people eat fondue together. We've found that the activity of cooking with the fondue forks helps people to relax even more.

At the end of the dinner, Gordon directs the men in clean-up operations. Again, people are drawn together around a *task*. All the merriment and teamwork make for an enjoyable evening and pave the way for vigorous discussion after the meal.

On occasion, we've asked people to bring one special item to our home. The object should weigh less than fifty pounds and should be something they would not like to be without on a trip to Europe. The emphasis is on the guests having something in hand when they arrive.

Another variation is having each guest bring one item that symbolizes a certain quality of marriage or vocation they admire or appreciate in some way. Later during the evening, each guest is given the chance to share his or her item.

If you happen to be entertaining people who don't know each other well, a circle game for twenty-five people or less could be an ideal ice-breaker. One person begins by giving his name and one sentence which describes something interesting about himself. The next person must repeat the first person's name and sentence description verbatim. The last few people in the circle will obviously have the biggest challenge of remembering! Tension and hilarity will mount as people attempt to remember names and descriptions. It's almost guaranteed that people in a group like that will be strangers no longer!

In entertaining groups of ten or twelve, Gordon and I have often split the guests into groups of four. Each group is then given an electric frying pan and the directions for cooking Japanese sukiyaki. We insist that the men do the cooking with some help from the women, if necessary. I provide colorful, frilly aprons for the men—any reserve they have had up to that point usually disappears!

I take care of providing the meat and vegetables for the sukiyaki, while each couple brings some other part of the meal—salad, rolls, dessert, etcetera. In this way, the burden of the expense doesn't fall on one person or family.

One especially unusual get-together we had in Collinsville was when we entertained our church choir consisting of thirty people. I recruited several high school girls to serve as waitresses. We distributed menus to the guests, each of whom was told to pick the dishes in the order in which he or she wanted to eat them. The guests were also instructed to order a different utensil to be used for each part of the meal.

The only problem was that each of the foods and the utensils was listed under a musical name. For example, utensils were called "batons," "slurs," and "sharps." The various entrees were: "Royal Piginissimo" (ham) served with "flats" (scalloped potatoes); "Strings and Light Accents" (stringbeans and frozen fruit salad); "Arias Supreme" (cream puffs); "Embellishments and Encores" (relishes); and "Staff" (bread).

Soon some were eating the dessert first and the meat last.

Others were eating beans with knives and ham with spoons! Laughter filled the house as people discovered what they had ordered.

What have evenings like the ones described shown me? For one thing: that laughter and good times dispel the notion that liquor is indispensable to a memorable evening. More than once, we've seen friendships develop during such evenings, as well as the blossoming of personal faith in Jesus Christ.

There are times when Gordon and I will invite a few individuals to our home after the Sunday evening service. These are usually part of the lay leadership. I'm partial to serving them "Make-your-own-hot-fudge-sundaes" since they're relatively easy to assemble. A simple, tasty food minimizes my labor and makes it possible for me to participate and reflect upon the way God has worked in the congregation that day.

On Wednesday evenings, Gordon will often entertain a "task" group in our living room. He insists that I serve nothing but tea or coffee since food preparation distracts from the purpose of having people in for a discussion. Also, elaborate and expensive food is not necessary to quality fellowship! It's a matter of deciding what's appropriate for the occasion. Incidentally, I usually serve decaffinated beverages in the evening.

I've also learned to use our home to get to know women I'm discipling or working with in our Bible study. By setting aside several easy-to-prepare salad and soup recipes in my recipe file, I've been able to whip up a tasty lunch and still have plenty of time to devote to the woman I've asked over for lunch. Conversation is ultimately far more important than the food we consume!

Let me point out that our home has become a place of increased hospitality since our children have grown older. Still, even when they were younger, we'd have a baby-sitter (usually Lynn Schmacker) who could keep them creatively occupied.

Never feel that a home is too simple, too unattractive, or too small to use for entertaining. Simplicity can be a witness in its own right. Orderliness and creative decor are more important than extravagance!

Congregations need to see pastors and spouses working together in their homes. Such teamwork authenticates what people hear and see during sermons and services. Pastors and their spouses are models—they can't get away from that! Members of a congregation may begin to follow their pastor's example and may open their homes to others. What they experienced when visiting the pastor's home may be duplicated in their own acts of hospitality.

I'm reminded of the hospitality given to our Lord by Mary, Martha, and Lazarus in the town of Bethany. And I can only speculate on the nature of the hospitality extended to Paul by Aquilla and Priscilla and Onesiphorus. One thing is certain: Paul relaxed and felt refreshed in the company of such people. We can assume that they had food to eat. Did they also play games and laugh?

Perhaps Jesus never played our circle name game, and Paul certainly never made sukiyaki in a frying pan. But I have no doubt that the hospitality they enjoyed was just as intense and just as effective as any hospitality loving Christians bring to others today. The experience of Christian hospitality helps everyone to grow. And growth is something *you* can encourage when you use your home. Being hospitable is not that difficult. I'm sure of that!

NOTES

CHAPTER 1
1. Oswald Chambers, *My Utmost for His Highest* (New York: Dodd, Mead & Co., 1935), p. 171.
2. Henri Nouwen, *Clowning in Rome* (Garden City, NY: Image Books, 1979), p. 41.

CHAPTER 2
1. Thomas à Kempis, *Of the Imitation of Christ: Selections* (Westwood, NJ: Fleming H. Revell Co., 1963), p. 22.
2. E. Herman, *Creative Prayer*, 5th ed. (Cincinnati: Forward Movement Publications, n.d.), p. 50.

CHAPTER 3
1. Ruth Graham, *Sitting at My Laughing Fire* (Waco, TX: Word, Inc., 1977), p. 26.
2. E. Herman, *Creative Prayer*, p. 16.

CHAPTER 4
1. E. Stanley Jones, *The Divine Yes* (Nashville: Abingdon Press, 1975), p. 70.

CHAPTER 5
1. Margaret Clarkson, *Grace Grows Best in Winter* (Grand Rapids: Zondervan Publishing House, 1975), p. 22.
2. Gordon MacDonald, *Magnificent Marriage* (Wheaton, IL: Tyndale House Publishers, Inc., 1977), p. 129.

CHAPTER 6
1. Findley Edge, *The Greening of the Church* (Waco, TX: Word, Inc., 1971), p. 141.

CHAPTER 7
1. Elisabeth Dodds, *Marriage to a Difficult Man: The Uncommon Union of Jonathan and Sarah Edwards* (Philadelphia: Westminster Press, 1971), p. 203.
2. John Pollack, *Hudson Taylor and Maria* (New York: McGraw-Hill Book Co., 1962), p. 102.

3. Clayton Bell, "A Look at Grief," *Leadership,* Vol. 1 (4), Fall, 1980: 42.
4. Ibid., p. 42.
5. Ibid., p. 51.
6. Norman Hapgood, *Daniel Webster* (Boston: Small, Maynard & Company, 1899), p. 64.
7. Ibid., p. 64.
8. Ibid., p. 64.
9. Elizabeth Skoglund, *Coping* (Glendale, CA: Regal Books, 1979), p. 28.
10. Ruth Graham, *Sitting at My Laughing Fire,* p. 106.

CHAPTER 8
1. Helen Smith Shoemaker, *I Stand by the Door* (Waco, TX: Word, Inc., 1977), p. 77.

CHAPTER 9
1. Thomas à Kempis, *Of the Imitation of Christ,* p. 44.
2. Ralph Turnbull, *A Minister's Obstacles* (Westwood, NJ: Fleming H. Revell Co., 1966), p. 38.

CHAPTER 10
1. E. Herman, *Creative Prayer,* pp. 38, 39.

CHAPTER 11
1. Elisabeth Dodds, *Difficult Man,* p. 78.
2. C. H. Mackintosh, "Notes on Exodus," in *Genesis to Deuteronomy: Notes on the Pentateuch.* (Neptune, NJ: Loizeaux Brothers, 1880, 1972), p. 155.
3. Dale E. Rogers, *Tears, Trials and Tribulations* (Old Tappan, NJ: Fleming H. Revell Co., 1977), p. 124.
4. E. Stanley Jones, *The Divine Yes,* p. 63.
5. Elizabeth Skoglund, *Coping,* p. 37.
6. Ibid., p. 37.
7. Ibid., p. 60.
8. Fred Bauer, *Springhouse Daily Devotional* (Glen Ellyn, IL: Springhouse Books, 1978), p. 126.

CHAPTER 12
1. Ralph Turnbull, *Minister's Obstacles,* p. 58.
2. Betty Thompson, ed., *The Healing Fountain: Writings Selected from Contemporary Christians* (New York: United Methodist Church, 1973), p. 146.
3. John Pollack, *Hudson Taylor and Maria,* p. 125.
4. Ibid., p. 102.

BIBLIOGRAPHY

WOMANHOOD

Hunt, Gladys. *MS Means Myself*. Grand Rapids: Zondervan Publishing House, 1975.

Ortlund, Anne. *The Disciplines of the Beautiful Woman*. Waco, TX: Word, Inc., 1977.

Petersen, Evelyn, and Petersen, J. Allan. *For Women Only*. Wheaton, IL: Tyndale House Publishers, Inc., 1975.

Price, Eugenia. *Woman to Woman*. Grand Rapids: Zondervan Publishing House, n.d.

Schaeffer, Edith. *Hidden Art*. Wheaton, IL: Tyndale House Publishers, Inc., 1975.

Trobisch, Ingrid. *The Joy of Being a Woman*. New York: Harper & Row Publishers, Inc., 1975.

RELATIONSHIPS

Angsburger, David. *The Freedom of Forgiveness*. Chicago: Moody Press, 1973.

Augsburger, David. *Caring Enough to Confront*. Glendale, CA: Regal Books, 1973.

Bonhoeffer, Dietrich. *Life Together*. New York: Harper & Row Publishers, Inc., 1976.

Dobson, James. *Dare to Discipline*. Wheaton, IL: Tyndale House Publishers, Inc., 1970.

_____. *Hide or Seek*. Old Tappan, NJ: Fleming H. Revell Co., 1974.

_____. *What Wives Wish Their Husbands Knew About Women*. Wheaton, IL: Tyndale House Publishers, Inc., 1977.

Drakeford, John. *The Awesome Power of the Listening Ear*. Waco, TX: Word, Inc., 1967.

Graham, Ruth. *Sitting at My Laughing Fire*. Waco, TX: Word, Inc., 1977.

Jacobs, Joan. *Feelings: Where They Come from and How to Handle Them*. Wheaton, IL: Tyndale House Publishers, Inc., 1976.

MacDonald, Gordon. *The Effective Father*. Wheaton, IL: Tyndale House Publishers, Inc., 1977.

_____. *Magnificent Marriage*. Wheaton, IL: Tyndale House Publishers, Inc., 1976.

Powell, John. *Why Am I Afraid to Love?* Niles, IL: Argus Communications, 1972.

Rogers, Dale Evans. *Tears, Trials and Tribulations*. Old Tappan, NJ: Fleming H. Revell Co., 1977.

Seamands, John T. *Healing for Damaged Emotions*. Wheaton, IL: Victor Books, 1981.

Tournier, Paul. *Secrets*. Atlanta: John Knox Press, 1976.

_____. *To Understand Each Other*. Translated by John S. Gilmour. Atlanta: John Knox Press, 1967.

Trobisch, Walter. *I Married You*. New York: Harper & Row Publishers, Inc., 1975.

John. *Parents in Pain*. Downers Grove, IL: Inter-Varsity Press, 1979.

Wright, H. Norman. *Communication: Key to Your Marriage*. Glendale, CA: Regal Books, 1979.

BIOGRAPHY AND AUTOBIOGRAPHY

Bentley-Taylor, David. *My Love Must Wait: The Story of Henry Martyn*. Downers Grove, IL: Inter-Varsity Press, 1976.

Dodds, Elisabeth. *Marriage to a Difficult Man: The Uncommon Union of Jonathan and Sarah Edwards*. Philadelphia: Westminster Press, 1971.

Elliot, Elisabeth. *Shadow of the Almighty*. Grand Rapids: Zondervan Publishing House, 1970.

Hapgood, Norman. *Daniel Webster*. Boston: Small, Maynard & Company, 1899.

Hopkins, Hugh. *Charles Simeon of Cambridge*. Grand Rapids: Wm. B. Eerdmans Publishing Co., 1977.

Jones, E. Stanley. *Song of Ascents: A Spiritual Biography*. Nashville: Abingdon Press, 1979.

Pollack, John. *Hudson Taylor and Maria*. Grand Rapids: Zondervan Publishing House, 1967.

Roseveare, Helen. *He Gave Us a Valley*. Downers Grove, IL: Inter-Varsity Press, 1976.

Schaeffer, Edith. *L'Abri*. Wheaton, IL: Tyndale House Publishers, Inc., 1969.

Shoemaker, Helen Smith. *I Stand by the Door*. Waco, TX: Word, Inc., 1967.

Trueblood, Elton. *While It Is Day*. New York: Harper & Row Publishers, Inc., 1974.

SUFFERING, DEATH, AND DYING

Bell, Clayton. "A Look at Grief." *Leadership* 1 (Fall, 1980): 40-51.

Clarkson, Margaret. *Grace Grows Best in Winter*. Grand Rapids: Zondervan Publishing House, 1975.

Hefley, James, and Hefley, Marti. *By Their Blood: Christian Martyrs of the Twentieth Century*. Milford, MI: Mott Media, 1978.

Hong, Edna. *Turn Over Any Stone*. Minneapolis, MN: Augsburg Publishing House, 1970.

Johnson, Margaret Woods. *We Lived with Dying*. Waco, TX: Word Books, 1975.

Jones, E. Stanley. *The Divine Yes*. Nashville: Abingdon Press, 1976.

Kübler-Ross, Elisabeth. *Questions and Answers on Death and Dying*. Riverside, NJ: Macmillan Publishing Co., Inc., 1974.

Landorf, Joyce. *Mourning Song*. Old Tappan, NJ: Fleming H. Revell Co., 1974.

Palmer, Bernard. *My Son, My Son.* Chicago: Moody Press, 1970.

Price, Eugenia. *No Pat Answers.* Grand Rapids: Zondervan Publishing House, 1975.

Schaeffer, Edith. *Affliction.* Old Tappan, NJ: Fleming H. Revell Co., 1978.

Skoglund, Elizabeth. *Coping.* Glendale, CA: Regal Books, 1980.

Vanauken, Sheldon. *A Severe Mercy.* New York: Harper & Row Publishers, Inc., 1977.

Yancey, Phillip. *Where Is God When It Hurts.* Grand Rapids: Zondervan Publishing House, 1977.

STRETCHING MIND AND SPIRIT

Adams, Lane. *How Come It's Taking Me So Long to Get Better?* Wheaton, IL: Tyndale House Publishers, Inc., 1975.

A'Kempis, Thomas. *Of the Imitation of Christ: Selections.* Westwood, NJ: Fleming H. Revell Co., 1963.

Bonhoeffer, Dietrich. *The Cost of Discipleship.* Riverside, NJ: Macmillan Publishing Co., Inc., 1967.

Bruce, Alexander B. *The Training of the Twelve.* Grand Rapids: Kregel Publications, 1971.

Chambers, Oswald. *My Utmost for His Highest.* New York: Dodd, Mead & Co., 1935.

Edge, Findley. *The Greening of the Church.* Waco, TX: Word, Inc., 1971.

Elliot, Elisabeth. *A Slow and Certain Light.* Waco, TX: Word, Inc., 1976.

Fenelon. *Let Go!* Springdale, PA: Whitaker House, 1973.

Foster, Richard J. *The Celebration of Discipline: Paths to Spiritual Growth.* New York: Harper & Row Publishers, Inc., 1978.

Gilkey, Langdon. *Shantung Compound.* New York: Harper & Row Publishers, Inc., 1975.

Herman, E. *Creative Prayer,* 5th ed. Cincinnati: Forward Movement Publications, n.d.

Keller, Phillip. *A Shepherd's Look at Psalm 23.* Grand Rapids: Zondervan Publishing House, 1976.

Minirth, Frank B., and Meier, Paul. *Happiness Is a Choice.* Grand Rapids: Baker Book House, 1978.

Muggeridge, Malcolm. *Christ and the Media.* Grand Rapids: Wm. B. Eerdmans Publishing Co., 1978.

Nouwen, Henri. *Clowning in Rome.* Garden City, NY: Image Books, 1979.

_____. *The Genesee Diary: Report from a Trappist Monastery.* Garden City, NY: Doubleday & Co., Inc., 1976.

Ortlund, Anne. *Up with Worship.* Glendale, CA: Regal Books, 1975.

Packer, James I. *Knowing God.* Downers Grove, IL: Inter-Varsity Press, 1973.

Sanders, J. Oswald. *Spiritual Leadership.* Chicago: Moody Press, 1974.

Sider, Ronald J. *Rich Christians in an Age of Hunger: A Biblical Study.* Ramsey, NJ: Paulist Press, 1977.

Tournier, Paul. *A Place for You.* New York: Harper & Row Publishers, Inc., 1968.

_____. *The Strong and the Weak.* Philadelphia: Westminster Press, 1976.

Tozer, A. W. *The Knowledge of the Holy.* New York: Harper & Row Publishers, Inc., 1978.

_____. *The Pursuit of God.* Harrisburg, PA: Christian Publications, Inc., 1948.

Turnbull, Ralph. *A Minister's Obstacles.* Westwood, NJ: Fleming H. Revell Co., 1966.

OTHER HELPS

Bauer, Fred. *Springhouse Daily Devotional*. Glen Ellyn, IL: Springhouse Books, 1978.

Hunt, Gladys. *Honey for a Child's Heart*. Grand Rapids: Zondervan Publishing House, 1969.

Le Bar, Lois E. *Family Devotions with School-Age Children*. Old Tappan, NJ: Fleming H. Revell Co., 1973.

LeFever, Marlene. *Creative Hospitality*. Wheaton, IL: Tyndale House Publishers, Inc., 1980.

Mackintosh, C. H. "Notes on Exodus." In *Genesis to Deuteronomy: Notes on the Pentateuch*. Neptune, NJ: Loizeaux Brothers, 1880, 1972.

Thompson, Betty, ed. *The Healing Fountain: Writings Selected from Contemporary Christians*. New York: United Methodist Church, 1973.

Other Living Books Best-sellers

THE ANGEL OF HIS PRESENCE by Grace Livingston Hill. This book captures the romance of John Wentworth Stanley and a beautiful young woman whose influence causes John to reevaluate his well-laid plans for the future. 07-0047 $2.95.

ANSWERS by Josh McDowell and Don Stewart. In a question-and-answer format, the authors tackle sixty-five of the most-asked questions about the Bible, God, Jesus Christ, miracles, other religions, and creation. 07-0021 $3.95.

THE BEST CHRISTMAS PAGEANT EVER by Barbara Robinson. A delightfully wild and funny story about what happens to a Christmas program when the "Horrible Herdman" brothers and sisters are miscast in the roles of the biblical Christmas story characters. 07-0137 $2.50.

BUILDING YOUR SELF-IMAGE by Josh McDowell. Here are practical answers to help you overcome your fears, anxieties, and lack of self-confidence. Learn how God's higher image of who you are can take root in your heart and mind. 07-1395 $3.95.

THE CHILD WITHIN by Mari Hanes. The author shares insights she gained from God's Word during her own pregnancy. She identifies areas of stress, offers concrete data about the birth process, and points to God's sure promises that he will "gently lead those that are with young." 07-0219 $2.95.

400 WAYS TO SAY I LOVE YOU by Alice Chapin. Perhaps the flame of love has almost died in your marriage. Maybe you have a good marriage that just needs a little "spark." Here is a book especially for the woman who wants to rekindle the flame of romance in her marriage; who wants creative, practical, useful ideas to show the man in her life that she cares. 07-0919 $2.95.

GIVERS, TAKERS, AND OTHER KINDS OF LOVERS by Josh McDowell and Paul Lewis. This book bypasses vague generalities about love and sex and gets right to the basic questions: Whatever happened to sexual freedom? What's true love like? Do men respond differently than women? If you're looking for straight answers about God's plan for love and sexuality, this book was written for you. 07-1031 $2.95.

HINDS' FEET ON HIGH PLACES by Hannah Hurnard. A classic allegory of a journey toward faith that has sold more than a million copies! 07-1429 $3.95.

HOW TO BE HAPPY THOUGH MARRIED by Tim LaHaye. One of America's most successful marriage counselors gives practical, proven advice for marital happiness. 07-1499 $3.50.

JOHN, SON OF THUNDER by Ellen Gunderson Traylor. In this saga of adventure, romance, and discovery, travel with John—the disciple whom Jesus loved—down desert paths, through the courts of the Holy City, to the foot of the cross. Journey with him from his luxury as a privileged son of Israel to the bitter hardship of his exile on Patmos. 07-1903 $4.95.

Other Living Books Best-sellers

KAREN'S CHOICE by Janice Hermansen. College students Karen and Jon fall in love and are heading toward marriage when Karen discovers she is pregnant. Struggle with Karen and Jon through the choices they make and observe how they cope with the consequences and eventually find the forgiveness of Christ. 07-2027 $3.50.

LIFE IS TREMENDOUS! by Charlie "Tremendous" Jones. Believing that enthusiasm makes the difference, Jones shows how anyone can be happy, involved, relevant, productive, healthy, and secure in the midst of a high-pressure, commercialized society. 07-2184 $2.95.

LOOKING FOR LOVE IN ALL THE WRONG PLACES by Joe White. Using wisdom gained from many talks with young people, White steers teens in the right direction to find love and fulfillment in a personal relationship with God. 07-3825 $3.50.

LORD, COULD YOU HURRY A LITTLE? by Ruth Harms Calkin. These prayer-poems from the heart of a godly woman trace the inner workings of the heart, following the rhythms of the day and the seasons of the year with expectation and love. 07-3816 $2.95.

LORD, I KEEP RUNNING BACK TO YOU by Ruth Harms Calkin. In prayer-poems tinged with wonder, joy, humanness, and questioning, the author speaks for all of us who are groping and learning together what it means to be God's child. 07-3819 $3.50.

LORD, YOU LOVE TO SAY YES by Ruth Harms Calkin. In this collection of prayer-poems the author speaks openly and honestly with her Lord about hopes and dreams, longings and frustrations, and her observations of life. 07-3824 $3.50.

MORE THAN A CARPENTER by Josh McDowell. A hard-hitting book for people who are skeptical about Jesus' deity, his resurrection, and his claims on their lives. 07-4552 $2.95.

MOUNTAINS OF SPICES by Hannah Hurnard. Here is an allegory comparing the nine spices mentioned in the Song of Solomon to the nine fruits of the Spirit. A story of the glory of surrender by the author of *HINDS' FEET ON HIGH PLACES*. 07-4611 $3.95.

THE NEW MOTHER'S BOOK OF BABY CARE by Marjorie Palmer and Ethel Bowman. From when to call the doctor to what you will need to clothe the baby, this book will give you all the basic knowledge necessary to be the parent your child needs. 07-4695 $2.95.

NOW IS YOUR TIME TO WIN by Dave Dean. In this true-life story, Dean shares how he locked into seven principles that enabled him to bounce back from failure to success. Read about successful men and women—from sports and entertainment celebrities to the ordinary people next door—and discover how you too can bounce back from failure to success! 07-4727 $2.95.

THE POSITIVE POWER OF JESUS CHRIST by Norman Vincent Peale. All his life the author has been leading men and women to Jesus Christ. In this book he tells of his boyhood encounters with Jesus and of his spiritual growth as he attended seminary and began his world-renowned ministry. 07-4914 $3.95.

Other Living Books Best-sellers

REASONS by Josh McDowell and Don Stewart. In a convenient question-and-answer format, the authors address many of the commonly asked questions about the Bible and evolution. 07-5287 $3.95.

ROCK by Bob Larson. A well-researched and penetrating look at today's rock music and rock performers, their lyrics, and their life-styles. 07-5686 $3.50.

SHAPE UP FROM THE INSIDE OUT by John R. Throop. Learn how to conquer the problem of being overweight! In this honest, often humorous book, Throop shares his own personal struggle with this area and how he gained fresh insight about the biblical relationship between physical and spiritual fitness. 07-5899 $2.95.

SUCCESS: THE GLENN BLAND METHOD by Glenn Bland. The author shows how to set goals and make plans that really work. His ingredients of success include spiritual, financial, educational, and recreational balances. 07-6689 $3.50.

TAKE ME HOME by Bonnie Jamison. This touching, candid story of the author's relationship with her dying mother will offer hope and assurance to those dealing with an aging parent, relative, or friend. 07-6901 $3.50.

TELL ME AGAIN, LORD, I FORGET by Ruth Harms Calkin. You will easily identify with Calkin in this collection of prayer-poems about the challenges, peaks, and quiet moments of each day. 07-6990 $3.50.

THROUGH GATES OF SPLENDOR by Elisabeth Elliot. This unforgettable story of five men who braved the Auca Indians has become one of the most famous missionary books of all times. 07-7151 $3.95.

WAY BACK IN THE HILLS by James C. Hefley. The story of Hefley's colorful childhood in the Ozarks makes reflective reading for those who like a nostalgic journey into the past. 07-7821 $3.95.

WHAT WIVES WISH THEIR HUSBANDS KNEW ABOUT WOMEN by James Dobson. The best-selling author of *DARE TO DISCIPLINE* and *THE STRONG-WILLED CHILD* brings us this vital book that speaks to the unique emotional needs and aspirations of today's woman. An immensely practical, interesting guide. 07-7896 $3.50.

YES by Ann Kiemel. In this window into Ann's heart, she tells—in her usual honest, charming way—how she has answered a resounding YES to Jesus in the various circumstances of her life. 07-8563 $2.95.

The books listed are available at your bookstore. If unavailable, send check with order to cover retail price plus $1.00 per book for postage and handling to:

Tyndale DMS
Box 80
Wheaton, Illinois 60189

Prices and availability subject to change without notice. Allow 4–6 weeks for delivery.